evolutionary economics

evolutionary economics

KENNETH E. BOULDING

 SAGE PUBLICATIONS   Beverly Hills   London

For information address:

SAGE Publications, Inc.
275 South Beverly Drive
Beverly Hills, California 90212

SAGE Publications Ltd
28 Banner Street
London EC1Y 8QE, England

Printed in the United States of America

Library of Congress Cataloging in Publication Data

Boulding, Kenneth Ewart, 1910-
   Evolutionary economics.

   Bibliography: p.
   Includes index.
   1. Economics. I. Title.
HB71.B659   330   81-8953
ISBN 0-8039-1648-5   AACR2
ISBN 0-8039-1649-3 (pbk.)

SECOND PRINTING, 1982

CONTENTS

About the Author

KENNETH E. BOULDING is truly one of the magisterial figures in the field of social science. The recipient of thirty honorary degrees and a variety of other awards, he has served as president of six major scholarly societies and taught at universities in seven countries. His hundreds of articles and pamphlets cover a broad range of topics, and he has written over thirty books, including the widely discussed *Ecodynamics*. With his wife Elise, he was a pioneer in the field of peace and conflict research. Currently, Boulding is Distinguished Professor of Economics Emeritus at the University of Colorado, and Director of the Program of Research on General Social and Economic Dynamics in the university's Institute of Behavioral Science.

INTRODUCTION

One of the striking things about the human race is that it has the capacity, which is now in considerable part realized, of developing an image of the whole universe as it spreads out in space and time. It is doubtful whether even the most intelligent nonhuman creature on earth has developed more than an image of its immediate environment or its own life-span. This extraordinary ability of the human race is in large measure a result of its capacity for interpreting the present structures of which it is aware as records of the past, for it is by interpreting these structures as records that we are able to build up in our minds images of the past, extending now perhaps 10 or 20 billion years. The record of the past is, of course, very imperfect. In the first place, it is only a minute part of the past which leaves records at all. Furthermore, the record of the past is not only a very small sample but an extremely biased one, biased by durability, for only what is durable in the past survives into the present. We build up our image of the past by our interpretation of these durables: light waves, hydrogen atoms, rocks, fossils, bones, prints, impressions, chipped flints, pots, ruins of buildings, shells, middens, durable human artifacts, inscriptions, papyri and scrolls, books and cassettes.

Out of these fragments of the past that have survived we construct images in our minds of the world or even the universe as a succession of constantly changing states through time. How we do this is still a bit of a puzzle. We have, in the first place, an enormous capacity for fantasy, for imagining worlds that we have not experienced; the innumerable myths of religions, the gods of Japan and of Olympus, the adventures of the Odyssey, the world of faerie and of midsummer night's dreams, the romantic and the gothic novel, and science fiction. Some of this we recognize as fantasy, some we believe to be truth.

The belief that a particular image is true may just come from authority. When we are children, we believe what our parents tell us, and even when we are adults, we believe what those in authority over us tell us. The other source of the belief that something is true is evidence, and that again is puzzling, as to what evidence is convincing and what is not. Evidence is what confirms or contradicts an image of the world. In some cases, evidence is easy and unambiguous. This is frequently the case in ordinary daily life. We have an image in our mind of our friend's house; we go there, we find it has burned down, we perceive therefore our image was untrue, and we revise it accordingly. Even in our daily life, however, evidence is ambiguous. What was it we ate that gave us a stomachache? What did I do to my wife that made her angry? The ambiguity of evidence is what gives the detective story its interest and the law its terrifying hold over us. Were Sacco and Vanzetti guilty?

In some cases we resolve the ambiguity of evidence by experiment. This has been very important in science. It only applies, however, to systems which are stable, repeatable, and divisible, such as chemical systems, in which, for instance, all hydrogen atoms are essentially similar. We cannot do experiments on unique events, and we cannot experiment on the past. We may probe its records experimentally, but otherwise all we can do is make records, collect durables, compare them, interpret them, and perceive inconsistencies between our image and the record. New records are discovered; new durables emerge, like Carbon-14; lost documents are discovered, like the Dead Sea scrolls; and our image of the past changes. It is always, however, very insecure, very fragmentary, and constantly subject to change.

Under these circumstances, it seems brash to talk about an evolutionary perspective. How can we possibly know anything about the enormous complexities of the past with the extremely meager and biased evidence that we have? Two considerations give us reason to go on being brash. One is the capacity of the human mind for perceiving not only logical necessities, the kind that are involved in mathematics, but also what might be called empirical necessities, or near-necessities, images of systems and relationships which "almost have to be that way." Many of the great laws of science are indeed truisms or near-truisms. They do not really require any empirical evidence, except perhaps in regard to the field of their application. Conservation laws are a good case in point. If there is a fixed quantity of anything, all we can do is push it around. A certain increase in one place must mean a corresponding decrease in other places. Even the famous second law of thermodynamics, the entropy principle, has this quality of being a near-truism, especially if we restate it in terms of negative entropy or potential, in which case it takes the generalized form that, if anything happens, it is because there is a potential for it happening, and after it has happened, that potential has been used up. A fundamental principle I call frivolously the "bathtub theorem" is really an example of the entropy law in very simple form, that the increase in the quantity of anything is equal to the additions minus the subtractions. This might almost be called the basic law of population, and again it is an identity.

The principle of ecological interaction is the first foundation of the evolutionary perspective. It is also in structure very close to being a truism. We define an ecosystem as a system of interacting populations of different kinds or species. Then we suppose that the additions to and subtractions from, and therefore, the rate of growth of the population of any one species depends upon, or in mathematical terms is a function of, the size of all the populations in the ecosystem, including its own. Essential to the existence of an ecosystem is the law of eventually diminishing growth of any one population as its size increases. As the population of any species grows, its rate of growth will decline until eventually it is zero, at which point the population is said to be in equilibrium and is occupying a "niche." Here, again, this is what might be called an empirical truism in the sense that if it were not so for any species, its population would expand forever until it filled a continually expanding universe. The law of diminishing returns in economics is a special case of this empirical truism, proof of which is that if it were not so, we could grow all of the world's food in a flower pot, and everybody knows this is absurd. An empirical truism, therefore, might almost be defined as a proposition which, if it were not true, would lead to absurdity.

The evolutionary perspective supposes, therefore, that at any one moment in time or space there will be an ecosystem and that with a given set of parameters this will move to an equilibrium at which the rate of growth of all populations in it is zero. In some places this equilibrium is remarkably stable, for the parameters are stable. On the surface of the moon, for instance, the interaction of its various rocks has virtually ceased. It had changed very slowly indeed over at least 3 billion years, apart from the impact of an occasional meteorite, until the intrusion of the human race, the garbage of which may well be around for another 3 billion years. On earth, however, the evidence suggests that ecosystems have been extremely unstable and have undergone constant and irreversible change in their parameters. This is because of the development of life and therefore of populations of species which are self-reproducing and which have constant additions and subtractions.

On the moon the population of rocks suffered neither addition nor subtraction, so they are very stable, apart from an occasional addition from outer space. With the advent of DNA, on earth, with its two extraordinary properties of self-reproduction and of organizing the growth of reproducing phenotypes, a process of extraordinary irreversible change began on the earth, which is *bioevolution*. The principle evidence for this, of course, is fossil remains, which can be dated, at least approximately, by their position in the sequence of rocks and now, of course, to some extent by radioactive dating.

Bioevolution is characterized by constant ecological interaction, which is *selection*, under conditions of constant change of parameters, which is *mutation*. Some of the parametric change is physical, such as changes in climate, ice ages, soil erosion, mountain building, flooding, tides, and so on. The basic source of change in the biological parameters, however, is genetic mutation, that is, change in the structure of the genetic instructions contained in DNA with consequent change in the nature of the individuals of species which these genetic instructions produce.

The record of the rocks suggests something more than mere change, for we also detect a directionality, a "time's arrow." The earliest forms of life seem to have been something like viruses, then one-celled organisms like bacteria that did not leave many durable traces, though these are beginning to be discovered. The next great step was the development of many-celled organisms, beginning with plants. These begin to leave more traces, for even soft and perishable structures leave imprints in mud, which then hardens and thus are preserved. Then come animals in enormous variety, invertebrates, insects with exoskeletons, then the vertebrates with internal skeletons, and so on.

We seem to be able to trace several directionalities here. One is an increase in the size of the individual organism from the minute viruses to the blue whale, which seems to be the largest living thing that ever existed. This increase in size is the result of an increase in certain kinds of complexity. Complexity is a difficult concept to reduce to any kind of linear scale, yet we have little doubt that the human being is more complex than a virus or the amoeba. An element of this complexity is the development of what might be called control or cybernetics; the development of, for instance, improved perceptual apparatus, from the slightly light-sensitive skin to the eye, from a vague sensitivity to air waves to the ear. We see control developing also in warm-bloodedness and with the development of a large number of cybernetic systems within the organism which sustain the stable internal environment in the face of changing external environments. Pleasure and pain make up another aspect of control, for this leads into behavior, which sustains the internal environment of the organism and improves eating, drinking, breathing, and avoiding predators.

The invention of sex, which comes fairly early, is certainly part of the increasing complexity. This leads to a speeding up of genetic change because in sexual reproduction individuals share the genes of both parents; this leads to larger and more complex gene pools in the species, greater variations in individual organisms, more rapid spread of favorable mutations through the species, an increased variability in behavior patterns among species because of the ever-present problem of getting the males and females together. I must confess that I am still a little puzzled as to why sex turned out to be such a good idea, as against asexual reproduction, but the answer is presumably that it permitted an enormous increase in the complexity of the organism. It would certainly be hard to see how asexual reproduction could work beyond the level of the cell, or at least the worm. It is certainly hard to imagine the human being dividing into two halves, and then each half growing into a complete person.

The last "time's arrow" in evolution is the development of awareness, consciousness, and intelligence. It seems almost impossible to pinpoint the moment at which this emerges, as it does so almost imperceptibly out of control and out of the pain and pleasure elements in control. Wordsworth may just have been a romatic poet when he wrote: "and 'tis my faith that every flower enjoys the air it breathes."[1] But the only evidence for the existence of pain in other organisms and in ourselves is the observation of behavior which is similar to our own when we feel pain, as no one has ever felt the pain of another directly. The same presumably goes for pleasure. When an amoeba rejects a stone and accepts food or a sunflower turns its face toward the sun as it moves across the sky, we seem to run into a phenomenon of preference, though the thermostat does almost as well without any feelings involved.

There is nothing impossible about an organism that could feel pain but could not express it. Boiling a carrot alive certainly produces less empathy in us than boiling a lobster, and much less than boiling another person, because of differences in expressiveness.

Two empirical processes tend to confirm our image of the pattern of evolution. One is the importance of negative evidence. We have never found the skeleton of a mammal in the Cambrian rocks, or the remains of an automobile in any human deposit of more than a hundred years ago. Negative evidence is always theoretically a little insecure, and if we found the remains of a spaceship and an extraterrestrial being in some part of the world entombed in ancient mud, it would radically change our image of the past. Still, until it is contradicted, negative evidence has to be taken very seriously. And the negative evidence for the evolutionary arrow is very strong; in fact, up to now, indubitable.

A second empirical clue is the parallel between the records and durable deposits which are made by existing systems and the durable deposits of the past. The fact that oysters exist in the present means that when we find an old oyster shell we have a very strong suspicion that it was an oyster that produced it. If we discovered a planet on which life was extinct but had left a fossil record, we would find this record much harder to interpret than the one we find on our own planet.

The question of what it is in the system of evolution which gives us a directionality or a "time's arrow" in these various dimensions is a difficult question and by no means fully answered. Why, for instance, did the process of mutation and selection in biological organisms not produce a genetic equilibrium long ago in which all mutations were adverse? There may well have been times in the evolutionary process when biological change was very slow and something like a genetic equilibrium seems almost to have been reached. A very interesting question here is the role of catastrophe in the process of evolution. Certainly some kind of catastrophe is indicated when one geological era gives place to the next. There are frequently extinctions of large species and then a sudden burst of evolutionary development.

An important concept here is that of the "empty niche"—that is, a species that would have a positive population in an ecosystem if it existed. If an empty niche is filled, of course, whether by mutation or by migration, this changes all the other niches in the system, expanding some and contracting others, with perhaps some old populations going to zero and becoming extinct. It is clear, for instance, that presettlement Mauritius had empty niches for pigs and humans, and that once they arrived, the niche of the dodo shrank to zero. The directionality of the evolutionary process can be explained, in part at any rate, by the hypothesis that there are more likely to be empty niches at the "top"—that is, for species of greater complexity, control, or consciousness, than there are at the bottom, where the niches for the simpler species are likely already to have been filled. Once a mutation fills an empty niche at the top, however, this may create empty niches for still more complex species, as the "top" itself expands.

Once biological evolution had produced the human race, a whole new pattern set in, though very slowly at first. We can trace creations of evolutionary potential in the past, such as the development of DNA and life itself, the transition of anaerobic to aerobic organisms, transition to multicellular organisms, the development of sex, the movement from sea to land, the development of the vertebrate skeleton, and so on. The coming of the human race is unquestionably one of these. With this, evolution went into a new gear in terms of human artifacts. Human history, indeed, is the evolution of human artifacts, which are of three kinds. The first are "things"—material objects, from the first eolith and chipped flint, through clothing, houses, pottery, metal wares, and ships, to computers and space probes. Second, going along with these and assisting in their production, we have organizations, from the band and the tribe to the church, the corporation, the nation state, and the United Nations. Finally, these help to produce by a learning process new categories of persons and occupational specialists, from hunters and gatherers to farmers, to kings and computer programmers. Each of these artifacts is a species, each of them has a population, each of them interacts with many others and with biological artifacts, and the physical and chemical environment. Human artifacts are as much a part of the world ecosystem as are tuberculosis bacteria and rabbits. The same principles of ecological interaction under constant change of parameters continue to apply. The same principle that there are likely to be empty niches for artifacts of greater complexity, control, and perhaps eventually consciousness, also applies.

There are, of course, important differences between societal and biological evolution. Each new phase of evolution introduces new elements into the overall system of change. Thus, the genetic information which produces biological artifacts is contained in the organisms themselves. The genetic information which produces human artifacts is contained in human beings, human organizations, and material artifacts which are different from the ones produced. With the advent of the human race something that might almost be called "super sex" came into evolution, whereas biological evolution never got beyond two sexes. The production of human artifacts is "multiparental," in the sense that the genetic information which organizes the production of human artifacts is contained not just in two other artifacts, but in very large numbers of artifacts of great vareity—human beings themselves, blueprints, libraries, computers, and so on. This undoubtedly is the main reason why the development of human artifacts enormously speeded up the pace of evolution, just as the development of biological sex speeded it up, simply because of the enormous increased potential not only for change and variety but also for the spread of the genetic information which organizes the production of artifacts. The "gene pool" of human artifacts is the whole sphere of human knowledge in brains, books, and computers spread over the face of the earth.

The development of human consciousness also enormously changes the process of evolution. Biological evolution proceeds on the whole by unconscious interaction and nondialectical processes. Two species, for instance, can be ecologically competitive or cooperative without either of them being the slightest degree aware of the other. There is little conscious interaction in the biosphere, except in sexual selection, in predation, and the avoidance of predation. This rises in importance with the higher animals, but it is still fairly minor in its effects. With the human race, conscious interaction becomes of great importance and the niches for human artifacts are determined in part by consciousness, for instance by the demand for them and by human images of the future.

Finally, we come to economics, with which this book is mainly concerned. Economic life is essentially a subset, and a fairly large one at that, of total human activity in history. We should expect it, therefore, to follow the general principles which govern the evolution of humans and human society, and we should also expect it to have some peculiarities of its own. Economics deals with that portion of human activity, as we shall see, which deals with the production, consumption, distribution, and exchange of economic goods. To this old taxonomy, I would add storage and enjoyment of stocks of economic goods, with production and consumption being merely the additions to and the subtractions from these stocks. We can think of economic goods, therefore, as part of the general ecosystem of the world. Any good with an existing stock clearly has a niche of some sort, although that may be ve y temporary. Then the ecological interaction provides a selective mechanism. In the case of economic goods, this is very powerfully affected by the attitudes of human beings toward them. Thus, an economic good for which there is no demand will have no niche in the system. Mutation in economic goods consists of the constant invention of new ones. This has gone on from the beginning of the human race. Many of these new goods do not find a niche and do not survive; others have a niche and expand into the system, with consequent changes in all the other niches.

In the case of economic goods the ecological interaction is mediated strongly through the price system, as we shall see. It is also mediated by such things as populations of financial instruments which exhibit interest rates, profit rates, and so on. These have little or no counterpart in the biosphere. We also find phenomena like unemployment, labor markets, inflation, and so on, which, again, have no counterpart in the biosphere. Nevertheless, we shall find the evolutionary perspective extremely illuminating in explaining the ongoing processes of economic life and its political and social environment. Economics has rested too long in an essentially Newtonian paradigm of mechanical equilibrium and mechanical dynamics. Oddly enough, as we shall see, economics had something to do with developing the evolutionary perspective. In a very real sense, Adam Smith and Malthus were evolutionary theorists, and so was Alfred Marshall. It was Walras and his successors who mathematicized so successfully the Newtonian system that the evolutionary perspective was lost. This little volume is intended to provide at least a prospectus for its rediscovery.

Social Darwinism

We should not leave the general subject of the evolutionary perspective without a brief glance at the movement of thought in the late nineteenth and early twentieth centuries that went by the name of "Social Darwinism." This was indeed an attempt to apply the evolutionary perspective, as its practitioners saw it, to social systems. It is particularly associated with the name of Herbert Spencer in the United

Kingdom, and W. G. Sumner in the United States.[2] It unfortunately incorporated a profoundly erroneous view of the nature of evolution in its theoretical structure. It gave evolutionary theory a bad name, especially in sociology, from which it has taken a long time to recover. Its major error was that it completely underestimated the complexity of ecological interaction which is involved in the selection process. It laid too much stress on the competitive aspects of natural selection, which it used to justify in social systems politics of unbridled competition and to deny the role of government and political structure in the social evolutionary process.

Darwin was certainly not a Social Darwinist, but perhaps he is somewhat to blame, if only for his use of metaphors which are easily misunderstood. The principle, for instance, of "the survival of the fittest," which actually was borrowed by Darwin from Herbert Spencer, was easily interpreted to mean survival of an aggressive, macho-type mentality at the expense of the more cooperative and accomodating patterns of behavior. As even Thomas Huxley[3] showed, "the survival of the fittest" is a quite empty principle, simply because if we ask "Fit for what?" the answer is "To survive," so that all we have is a survival of the surviving, which we knew anyway, and unless fitness—that is, survival value—can be specified in some way, the principle is quite empty. In fact fitness in this sense is enormously complex. Ecosystems have innumerable niches for different kinds of creatures and behaviors. A much better phrase would be "the survival of the fitting," that is, the species that fits into a niche in an ecosystem, and these niches can be very various indeed. Kropotkin,[4] and later Clyde Allee,[5] showed very convincingly that in biological evolution, cooperative behavior often paid off very well, and indeed the principle of "the survival of the fitting" can easily be translated into the principle that the meek—that is, the adaptable— inherit the earth. The tough and the unadaptable either kill each other off or do not survive changes in the environment.

Another very unfortunate metaphor of Darwin's was "the struggle for existence." In fact, ecological interaction involves very little struggle in the sense of organized and conscious fighting, or even very much organized endeavor. Ecological interaction is through birth and death, and the subtle impact of large numbers of variables on these quantities. Struggle is a relatively minor aspect of ecological interaction, found somewhat in sexual selection, where quite often, as a matter of fact, it leads to extinction. Traits which are selected for by fighting among the males are by no means those which lead to the survival of the species as a whole. It is a very fundamental principle that traits which propagate through a particular species may easily diminish its niche in the overall ecosystem.

This is not of course to deny the importance of competitive relationships in ecological systems, and also in social systems. Evolution proceeds indeed by the endangering and the eventual extinction of species and their replacement by others that find niches. Nature is only occasionally "red in tooth and claw," which worried Tennyson so much. The complexity of habitats means that competition in ecosystems is extremely imperfect and that a species threatened with decline in its niche often retreats to some protected habitat where the decline is arrested, sometimes for a very long time, from which it sometimes emerges again when conditions are favorable. We find the same thing happening in society, where persecution, for instance, or conquest may drive a particular people or culture underground or to the hills, where they survive until in some sense they emerge as the system changes. This husbanding of genetic material is an important principle in the evolutionary process.

Social Darwinism was particularly attacked because it seemed to justify a rip-roaring unfettered capitalism at a time when the socialist message was finding many sympathetic ears, especially among social scientists. The evolutionary perspective, however, properly interpreted, stands curiously above this particular conflict. An individual organism—the chicken, for instance—is a centrally planned economy. Its growth and development are planned from the very beginning by the genetic information and instructions contained in the fertilized egg. Studies of identical twins that have been separated from birth or early childhood suggest that even in human beings the genetic information in the original fertilized egg plays a remarkable role in our individual history and development, even of tastes, though of course by no means a determining one. "The best laid schemes o' mice an' men gang aft a-gley," as Burns[6] said, even in fertilized eggs.

On the other hand, an ecosystem is a free private enterprise beyond the dreams of Milton Friedman. Biologists call an ecosystem in a particular habitat a "community," but this is an absurd metaphor. No ecosystem outside the human race ever had a mayor. Whatever "plan" may be detected is generated by the unconscious interaction of the species within the ecosystem. The evolutionary perspective does suggest that there are very important limits to the size of planned systems, whether corporations or communist states. Evolution does not produce one living dragon coiled around the face of the earth. If it ever had done so, the dragon would have died. The persistence of evolution and its whole course depends very much on the free private enterprise aspects of it and on the fact that while individuals are planned to die, the whole system continues through billions of years with ongoing development, as we have seen. It could well be that in the evolutionary perspective planned economies of the size of General Motors, the U.S. Department of Defense, the Soviet Union, and the People's Republic of China are too large for efficiency, and their demise may be unconsciously and unexpectedly in the plan itself; but that is a matter of speculation.

Perhaps the greatest challenge to the evolutionary perspective is the dialectical perspective, the view that sees the long processes of the history of the universe as essentially conflicts between mutually hostile and opposing systems, each of which arises out of the contradictions of the other. The conflict may be resolved in a synthesis according to both Hegel and Marx, but this in turn is likely to produce a new synthesis, and so the struggle goes on. The evolutionary perspective does not deny the existence of dialectical processes. It does suggest, however, that in biological evolution they are relatively insignificant. As we move into societal evolution, with the appearance of the human race, dialectical processes do become more important. But they are still relatively minor compared with the processes of mutation and ecological interaction. It is only on rare occasions, what I have called "evolutionary watersheds," that a dialectical process may push a society into one watershed or another, as, for instance, the Russian Revolution pushed the society into a centrally planned economy, which failed in the Western countries.

There is even some question as to how important in the long run these watershed processes are. A great struggle on the watershed between the North and South Platte Rivers in Colorado might push some people into the valley of the North Platte and others into the valley of the South Platte, but they will all end up in Nebraska anyway. A similar struggle on the Continental Divide might be much more significant in the long run. These if's and and's of history, however, are very speculative and hard to determine. What is clear is that the evolutionary perspective puts dialectical theory as a special case of a more general system and marks it for further study. It is ironic that Marx asked Darwin if he could dedicate *Das Kapital* to him, which Darwin very wisely refused. For his own peace of mind, it is probably just as well that Marx never realized how devastatingly different the evolutionary vision, which owes so much to Darwin, is from the Hegelian dialectic, which colored so much of Marx's own thought.

So much for the setting of this volume. Chapter 1 explores the basic evolutionary model itself in more detail. Chapter 2 shows how the world of commodities, which is the main subject of economics, is itself an evolutionary system. Chapter 3 traces the evolutionary perspective back to Adam Smith and to classical economics and argues that it is in a sense a return to a more fundamental tradition after a "Newtonian" episode in the last 100 years. Chapter 4 explores the evolutionary approach to economic history in more detail. Chapter 5 takes on the question of the role of energy and entropy in evolutionary systems, especially as applied to economics. And Chapter 6 explores the policy implications of the evolutionary perspective in economics from the general point of view of the chances for human betterment.

NOTES

1. William Wordsworth, "Lines Written in Early Spring."
2. Richard Hofstadter, *Social Darwinism in American Thought* (Boston: Beacon Press, 1955; rev. ed., New York: Braziller, 1959) is an excellent account of the movement.
3. Thomas H. Huxley, *Evolution and Ethics* (1893); reprinted in Thomas H. and Julian Huxley, *Touchstone for Ethics: 1893-1943* (New York: Harper, 1947).
4. Peter Kropotkin, *Mutual Aid: A Factor in Evolution* (New York: Doubleday, 1902).
5. W. Clyde Allee et al., *Principles of Animal Ecology* (Philadelphia: Saunders, 1949).
6. Robert Burns, "To a Mouse."

CHAPTER 1

The Basic Evolutionary Model

The Evolution of Evolutionary Thought

In 1898 Thorstein Veblen published his famous paper entitled "Why Is Economics Not an Evolutionary Science?"[1] The answer I think at that time was clear, although Veblen did not give it. In 1898 there was not very much evolutionary science, and even what there was, unfortunately, Veblen did not understand very well. What he was really looking for was a kind of celestial mechanics of society, a set of stable parameters uniting events of successive time periods. This kind of theory has indeed developed in the last few decades, particularly in the form of the application of difference equations and econometric dynamic models to the study of economic life, but this is not really what is meant by evolution. My own definition of evolution is that it consists of ongoing ecological interaction, of populations of species of all kinds which affect each other, under conditions of constantly changing parameters. These species and populations consist not only of biological species like robins and horses, but of physical species like water molecules or oxygen molecules, and social species like gas stations and automobiles. Ecological interaction, particularly as it is spread out in space as well as in time, is extremely complex, though simple models of it which assume, for instance, that each species has an equilibrium population which is a function of the size of all the other populations, have some usefulness. Since 1898 we have developed a good deal more evolutionary science, especially in the biological sciences, than we had then. In 1898, for instance, genetics was in its infancy; Mendel had barely been rediscovered, ecology as an organized discipline had still to come into existence, molecular biology lay well in the future, and the study of the development of individual organisms from their fertilized eggs or other origins was still very primitive. Since then substantial advances have been made in all these fields and it may be, therefore, that the time has come to take another look at economics, to see in the first place if it has anything to contribute to evolutionary science, and in the second place to see if evolutionary science has anything to contribute to it.

Economics as Studying the Provision, Exchange, and Transfer of Goods

Economics centers on the study of how society is organized through the provision, exchange, and transfer of commodities or economic goods. The definition of economic goods, like all important categories, is a little vague, but certainly clear enough to be useful, even though there may be some doubtful cases. Economic goods are an important subset of the total set of social species. There are three major categories of social species: things—that is, human artifacts, such as typewriters or automobiles; organizations, like families, national states, or corporations; and persons, insofar as the characteristics of persons are produced by interaction and communication with other persons and by the learning processes within the body of the person. Every human being is in part a biological artifact resulting from the information in the original fertilized egg, and in part a social artifact insofar as learned images, knowledge, and behavior, such as language, skills, and so on, are acquired in the course of life.

Economic goods consist mainly of human artifacts, "things"—shoes and ships and sealing wax and cabbages—though they also include the services of people as labor which is sold for wages, or even kings who are ransomed. They also include organizations, as, for instance, when a firm is bought or sold. In some societies they include people as slaves.

Production as Getting from the Genotype to the Phenotype

Individual "phenotypes," members of both biological and social species, including economic goods, come into being as a result of processes of production. Any individual member of any species, biological or social, at a moment of time, must be thought of as a cross section of its "life," a kind of four-dimensional "worm" in the space-time continuum, with a beginning at conception or production-plan and an end in death or destruction.

All processes of production, whether biological, social, or economic, originate in some kind of information structure or "know-how." In the biological individual this is the genetic information as it exists in its origin in the fertilized egg or divided cell. In social systems the genetic material consists of knowledge in the heads of persons, or in the blueprints, plans, libraries, or computers of organizations, including one-person organizations in the form of the single craftsman. If the product or phenotype is to be realized, this know-how or genetic information must be able to direct energy for three purposes: first, to maintain temperatures at which processes can be carried out, whether this is the blood temperature of the body or the heat of the kiln or the furnace; second, to do work in the form of transporting and transforming selected materials into the improbable structures of the phenotype; and third, to transmit information either as coded energy (nerve impulses, sound waves, telephones) or as coded materials (enzymes, hormones, documents, letters). These must also be the right materials, in the right quantities, capable of being transformed into the structure of the phenotype.

Biological and Social Species

Thus, the process by which a fertilized egg becomes a chicken is not essentially different from the process by which knowledge in the minds of automobile company members is transformed into an automobile. An automobile indeed is just as much an ecological species as a horse or a chicken; it is just as natural, just as much a product of the general process of evolution. There are major differences, however, between social and economic artifacts and biological artifacts or phenotypes. One difference is that whereas the biosphere never got beyond two sexes, with one or two possible exceptions, social artifacts are multiparental in the sense that the genetic information which underlies them is drawn from large numbers of different social species. Thus, a stallion and a mare can produce another horse in a bisexual union. An automobile, however, is produced as the result of the interaction of hundreds of different social species—mining equipment, lake steamers, steel mills, trucks, assembly lines, factories, and so on, on the material side; large numbers of organizations—different firms, social structures, and so on; and a great variety of different types of persons—miners, seamen, truck drivers, assembly line workers, executives, lawyers, policemen, and so on. They all come together, however, in an organized process which eventually produces the automobile in the womb of the factory, out of which it is born.

Another important difference between social and biological artifacts is that in the biological artifact the genetic instructions are carried in the artifact itself, at least in part. Thus, in organisms that have asexual reproduction, like the amoeba, the genetic instructions are contained in the cell itself, and when the cell divides the instructions are replicated and a complete set is found in each of the halves of the original cell. In sexual reproduction, all the genetic instructions are contained within each sex, with the exception that the male has a small deficiency, but the fertilized egg contains roughly half the genetic instructions of each parent. In the case of social artifacts, however, the genetic instructions are contained in other artifacts. Thus, the instructions for making an automobile are not contained within the automobile itself, but are contained in blueprints, computers, and so on of the automobile company. This is what makes the multiparental character of social artifacts possible, and it also contributes to the great rapidity of evolution in social artifacts, because the artifacts which contain the genetic instructions have become specialized and hence are particularly subject to change. In the horse there is not a new model every year—it takes a very long time to make one—unlike the automobile. A machine which contained the instructions and a program for making a replica of itself (like the "Türing Machine") is conceivable, but none have been made yet.

Another major difference between social and biological species is that biological species continue to grow after birth, although their eventual decay and death is written into the genetic instructions, whereas social species like automobiles begin to decay as soon as they are born and do not actually grow after they have been moved from the factory, although they do decay and eventually die by being scrapped. There are some possible exceptions to this rule—houses receive additions; even automobiles get reconstructed—and, of course, there is a large social apparatus for repair, which somewhat parallels the repair processes of simple organism biological organizations, by which cuts are healed, brain damage repaired; and even in some cases new heads, tails, or limbs may be grown to replace those lost. All repair involves the reapplication of genetic knowledge to the reconstruction of damaged artifacts.

The "Factors of Production" as Know-How, Energy, Materials, Not Land, Labor, and Capital

Looking at economics from an evolutionary point of view, one sees clearly that the traditional three "factors of production"—land, labor, and capital—are extremely unsatisfactory categories from the point of view of production. Alfred Marshall tried to solve this problem, without much success, by introducing a fourth factor, which he called organization. In this, as in many other ways, he was seeking for an evolutionary approach which he never quite mastered, again perhaps because of the primitive state of evolutionary science in the late nineteenth century.[2] It is much more accurate to identify the factors of production as know-how (that is, genetic information structure), energy, and materials, for, as we have seen, all processes of production involve the direction of energy by some know-how structure toward the selection, transportation, and transformation of materials into the product.

Each of the three traditional factors of production are varying combinations of know-how, energy, and materials. Labor, for instance, consists partly in the know-how in the nervous system of the laborer, both in the brain and in the lower nervous system of the muscles; partly in the energy of human muscles, powered ultimately by "burning" (oxidizing) food; partly in the materials which constitute the laborer. Capital consists of human artifacts, mainly though not exclusively material ones in the form of machines, buildings, and so on. These may contain know-how in themselves, as in automatic machinery. They may simply maintain temperatures at which human activity can be carried on, like buildings, furnaces, and thermostats. They may involve means of transporting materials or people, or of selecting and arranging parts into a complete object, like an automobile assembly line. They may involve the utilization of human knowledge or biological know-how, as in the development of domesticated animals and crops, and so on, in a very large variety of combinations of know-how, energy, and materials. Land, likewise, may involve mere space within which the activity of human beings and machines, or processes of shelter and heat maintenance, can be carried on. Or it may mean the capacity of the soil to provide materials and the sun to provide energy for the growing of crops.

Land, Labor, and Capital as Factors of Distribution, Not of Production

It is clear that land, labor, and capital are extremely heterogeneous aggregates from the point of view of the theory of production. In this respect they have all the scientific validity of the medieval elements of earth, air, fire, and water. They do, however, have significance as factors of distribution, simply because in an aggregate form they participate in the system of exchange and the distribution of income. A wage, for instance, is a price for the use of a certain amount of the services of a human being, so the concept of labor here makes sense. Similarly, the concept of rent per acre has significance in the exchange system. The concept of a rate of interest or a rate of profit has different dimensions from these, but also has some significance from the point of view of distribution of income. The idea of a production function of land, labor, and capital, however, is almost pure alchemy and has misled economists into many a vain search for empirical verification. Thus, attempts to relate the growth in the real product of society under processes of economic development to increases in land, labor, and capital must universally come up with a severe deficiency which has to be explained by a vague concept called "technology," which is something of a surrogate for "know-how." Increase in know-how continually changes the production functions—that is, changes the amount of product per unit of labor of some kind, or of capital of some kind, or of land of some kind. The whole concept of the traditional production function in which product is written as a function of the amount of inputs of land, labor, and capital is virtually useless except over very short periods.

Economic development is primarily a process in the increase of human know-how. This is strongly related, of course, to the increase in know-what, particularly as manifested in science. Materials and energy are limiting factors which may prevent the transformation of know-how into the product which the know-how knows how to make. The increase in know-how, however, has continually pushed back the boundaries at which these limiting factors come into play; for instance, in the discovery of fossil fuels, especially oil and natural gas, and in the discovery of new materials, like aluminum, titanium, and so on. This does not preclude the possibility that production may exhaust existing stocks of materials and energy. Historically, indeed, it has frequently done so; for instance, through soil exhaustion or erosion, or through the destruction of forests and exhaustion of mines. There is legitimate alarm at present as to whether the continued expansion of the human race and its products will not produce a crisis both of materials and of energy sharply limiting any further growth and leading to a decline within the next 100 or 200 years. This all depends, however, as it has done many times in the past, on the extent to which an increase in know-how can push back the limits of materials and energy, by finding new sources and new forms.

Space and Time as Limiting Factors

We perhaps should add two more factors of production—space and time—to the three previously mentioned, for all processes of production require these, and they also may be limiting factors. A population may be so crowded in space that it cannot produce enough of its own offspring. Space indeed operates as a limiting factor in two ways—having too much of it or too little. If processes are spread over too much space, the costs of transportation become a limiting factor. If there is too little space, crowding prevents the proper operation of the processes involved. Time, likewise, can be a limiting factor, because all processes take time and cannot be hurried beyond a certain point. Why they take time is an interesting question, to which there may be a number of answers. Sometimes this is a time pattern of chemical processes which is important, as in the maturing of wines. Sometimes it is the velocity of transportation, either of information or of materials, which is the limiting factor. Sometimes it is the time taken to remove obstacles, such as legal proceedings, licensing, and so on; or the removal of physical obstacles to the transportation of materials or energy. Increase in know-how can reduce these times. This would qualify as a "capital saving improvement" in terms of the old factors. An increase in know-how can also economize space in some circumstances. The development of the steel-frame building, for instance, permitted the building of skyscrapers, expanded the cities in the vertical dimension, and economized land. An increase in know-how which increases the yield of crops per acre likewise economizes space. Improvements in transportation have the same effect as a reduction in the limitation of space. The space limitation has an effect on the number of species and on the amount of interaction in social species; for instance, the amount of trade is increased with reduction in the cost of transportation. This means also that specialization may increase and productivity may increase in a very complicated positive feedback. This was recognized by Adam Smith in his famous Book I, Chapter 3, of *The Wealth of Nations.*

"Coevolution" of Cooperative or Symbiotic Species

The positive feedback processes in all patterns of evolution may be of great importance; this is "coevolution"—the opportunities for one species which are opened up by a change in another. The great expansion of the human race and of its artifacts in the last 10,000 years and the spectacular expansion of the last 200 years are a result essentially of a positive feedback process of this kind, whereby the human race becomes cooperative with its own artifacts and the artifacts are cooperative with the increase in knowledge and know-how, and therefore push back the limitations of the limiting factors. This is a process of great complexity which is hard to spell out in detail. It is found in biological evolution (symbiotic species, like the algae and fungus in lichen), and is of great importance in societal evolution at many levels.

Selection as Ecological Interaction

The basic concepts of mutation and selection apply to societal and economic evolution just as they do to biological evolution. In both cases selection is essentially the process of ecological interaction. The population of any species, whether of horses or of automobiles, grows if the additions to it exceed the subtractions. In the case of a biological population, the additions consist of births and the subtractions, deaths; or, if we are considering a subset of a population within a given area, additions consist of births plus inmigrations and subtractions consist of deaths plus outmigrations. The population (stock) of commodities likewise in any given area increases by production (births) and imports (inmigration) and decreases by consumption (deaths) and exports (outmigration).

Neglecting migration for the moment, the birth rate and the death rate of any population can be regarded as a function of its own size and the size of all relevant populations in its environment. If its environment is taken for the moment as fixed, the birth rate and the death rate can be treated as functions of the size of the population of the species in question. If a population increases in a given environment, the birth rate may increase somewhat at first because of higher population density; as population density increases, however, the birth rate may eventually decline because of the stresses of overcrowding. The relation between population and the death rate is likely to be more dramatic: As population increases, the death rate will eventually rise because of over-crowding, food shortages, increased predation, and so on, until at some equilibrium population the death rate and the birth rate are equal. This equilibrium population is the "niche" of the species. Usually this will be a stable equilibrium. If the population is below the equilibrium level, the birth rate will exceed the death rate and the population will rise; if it is above the equilibrium level, the death rate will exceed the birth rate and the population will fall. The introduction of migration increases the complexity of the system somewhat. A species, for instance, may have an excess of births over deaths and still be in equilibrium in a given area if this is counterbalanced by an excess of outmigration.

Ecological Equilibrium

An ecological equilibrium is a situation in which the population of each of the interacting species occupies a niche—that is, is neither rising nor falling. If we suppose that the equilibrium population for each species is a function of the actual population of all the others, this gives us n equations with n unknowns. These equations may have a real solution and, if they do, we have an equilibrium ecosystem in which each population is at the level of equilibrium which is consistent with the equilibrium level of all others. If there is any species for which the equilibrium population is not positive, the species will constantly decline; its death rate will be above its birth rate until it becomes extinct and the population is zero. This will then change the niches of all the other related species in the system. The processes of ecological dynamics, of course, are extremely complex. Especially in systems with rather small numbers of species, we can easily get fluctuations in populations, for instance, of predators and prey; and, if the amplitude of these is large enough, a population may become extinct through dynamic processes even though it could theroretically coexist in the niche with the others.

Mutation

Mutation in its most general form is the process by which the parameters of the system of ecological interaction change. In a simple model we can suppose that what changes is the parameters of the equations of ecological equilibrium, but the world is a dynamic system and equilibrium is very rarely attained, so that what is really significant is change in the parameters which affect the relationship between the total system and the birth and death rates of any given population. There are several forms of these mutational changes. In the biosphere, for in-stance, they may take the form of climatic changes, erosion or deposition of soils, the filling up of lakes, and so on. They also take the form of genetic mutations. These go on all the time. Usually they are adverse to the individual and the individuals possessing these mutations die out without this much affecting the species. Occasionally, however, they are favorable and there is a change in the gene pool of the species.

Successful mutation ordinarily may be expected to increase the niche of the species—that is, to permit it to have a larger stable population in a given environment. It is not inconceivable, however, that a mutation which is favorable to the survival of the changed (mutated) individuals of the species relative to the unchanged ones, may be adverse to the total species and result in a diminution of the niche. The niche of one species cannot change without changing the niches of all the others in the ecosystem. If it rises, some may change favorably, those, for instance, which are cooperative with the first species. Some may be affected unfavorably, those which are competitive with the first species. If the unfavorable change is sufficient, a species may become extinct. This is essentially how selection operates.

In the biosphere, in spite of Darwin's unfortunate metaphor about the struggle for existence, struggle in the sense of organized fighting, or even goal-oriented activity, plays very little role in the selection process. Selection essentially is a process of ecological interaction which takes place along many different lines—predation, symbiosis, competition for a common food supply, and so on. The situation is greatly complicated by the fact that the terrain on which biological interaction takes place is very heterogeneous. The interaction of species does not take place equally at all points in it. Heterogeneity often provides "shelters" for species within which they can survive, where they might not be able to survive out in the larger ecosystem. This is important in general evolutionary theory because the existence of these heterogeneities and shelters increases the variety of the total gene pool, which may affect the ultimate history of the evolutionary process. When conditions become more favorable outside the shelter, a sheltered species may emerge and occupy a larger habitat.

Ecosystems of Social Species

Looking now at social species, and especially the species of economic commodities, we see much the same principles at work, with, however, some additional complexities. The stock of any commodity is its population; production, as we have seen, corresponds to births and consumption to deaths. There is a little semantic problem here in that the term consumption has frequently been used in economics to mean simply household purchases, as if the commodity disappeared into a tomb once it entered the doors of the household. It is more realistic to regard consumption as the destruction of a commodity; in this case it becomes exactly parallel to death in the case of a biological species. Again, production and consumption are likely to be functions of the stock of the commodity—that is, of the population of the species. In the case of economic goods, however, this relationship is mediated mainly through the system of relative prices.

There is no exact counterpart to a price structure in the biosphere, though each species does have certain rates of exchange of materials and energy with its environment, and, if the situation is to be a true equilibrium, there must be "recycling" as we find in things like the nitrogen cycle and the carbon cycle. The symbiosis of plants and animals, for instance, on which the complexity of the biosphere so much depends, is in part a result of the fact that animals take in oxygen and give out carbon dioxide, while plants, in sunlight at least, take in carbon dioxide and give out oxygen. There is something here like a balance of trade and indeed the disturbance of this may have had some evolutionary consequences, as, for instance, in the carboniferous era when presumably plant life was so vigorous that it captured a great deal of the CO_2 from the atmosphere, changed its composition and probably its temperature, and hence created a change in the ecological equilibrium, which may have destroyed the whole carboniferous ecosystem. Similar things can easily happen in an economy, for instance, that is dependent on exhaustible resources—like our present economy!

Specialization, Exchange, and Relative Prices

Economic systems are characterized by the specialization of persons in the production of different commodities. Material artifacts and organizations are also specialized in this way, so that we have groups of persons, organizations, and artifacts specialized, for instance, in the production of wheat or steel. Commodities then are exchanged for each other, the exchange being enormously facilitated by the existence of money as a medium of exchange, as a store of value, and as a liquid asset. The wheat producer sells the wheat that is produced for money. This is distributed among all those who contributed to the production of the wheat and with the money these persons can buy clothing, furniture, automobiles, and so on, which are produced by other groups. A very important characteristic of such a system is the relative price structure; the price of each commodity, for instance, can be expressed in terms of a monetary unit such as a dollar, and this list immediately enables us to calculate the rate at which any one commodity can be exchanged for any other. If wheat is $4 a bushel, and an automobile costs $4000, then 1000 bushels of wheat can be exchanged for one automobile.

The relative price structure is an extremely important factor in determining the structure of the distribution of real income among the persons participating in the economy, because the relative price structure determines each person's terms of trade—that is, how much he gets per unit of what he gives in exchange. A rise in the price of any one commodity such as wheat, for instance, will redistribute real income toward wheat producers and away from the producers of all the things that wheat producers buy. Corresponding to any relative price structure, therefore, there is a structure of the distribution of real income.

An Equilibrium Price Structure

Economists postulate the existence of an equilibrium price structure such that the corresponding distribution of real income will not induce anyone to change their occupations to produce less of one commodity and more of another. This corresponds very closely to the idea of ecological equilibrium. The connecting link here is that the relative price structure under given conditions of demand is a function of the relative stocks of the different commodities. A rise, for instance, in the relative stock of wheat is likely to cause a decline in its market price, and a fall in the stock, an increase in the price. Exchange always involves the redistribution of existing stocks among owners and in any given distribution of demand for these stocks there will be some set of relative prices at which on balance people are willing to hold what is there to be held. If the relative price set is different from this equilibrium set, some prices will be perceived as "too high"; there will be on balance an excess offered for sale over what is purchased, and these prices will fall. Other prices will be perceived as "too low," there will be an excess of offers to purchase over offers for sale, and these prices will rise. The situation is complicated in practice by the fact that the demand for holding stocks of various commodities depends on the expectation of the change in their prices, so that we get speculative changes which may not correspond to the long-run equilibrium.

The structure of demand is of great importance in explaining the survival of commodities and the size of the "niche" (equilibrium stock) of each. This is something for which there is no exact counterpart in the biosphere, where there are really no decisions about exchange. Demand, as we have seen above, may depend in part on speculative expectations about future price changes. These average out in the long run and ultimately, apart from these disturbances, the structure of demand is a function of human tastes and preferences. These in turn are in large part learned and depend on the learning processes of a culture and may even depend in part on the price structure itself. There is, for instance, what might be called the "diamonds" phenomenon by which a certain item becomes demanded *because* it has a high price and is therefore a symbol of affluence and conspicuous consumption. In spite of these exceptions, however, there is a rather fundamentally basic structure of human demands, which varies considerably from culture to culture but nevertheless exhibits strong common patterns, in spite of vagaries of vanity and fashion. A commodity for which the demand is not large enough to generate production of it, under a price structure which will return adequate income to its producers, will not survive. Even if it exists, its production will decline below its consumption and the stocks will shrink until it becomes virtually extinct or fossilized, like sedan chairs or primitive hand-cranked computers.

Social and Economic Mutation

Mutations in the economic system and in the social system may be on the supply or the demand side. On the supply side they generally consist of invention and innovation; that is, the development of new social genetic structures involving new ideas, new forms of know-how, and, if mutations are favorable, new products and new social species occupying newly created niches. These new products, as they are produced, interact with the old species and may drive some of them to extinction, though they may also expand the niches of some old commodities which are cooperative with the innovation and may even create new niches which are at present empty, waiting for mutations to come. The discovery of oil in 1859 and the production of cheap gasoline (originally as an unwanted by-product of kerosene!) opened up an enormous niche for the automobile which was gradually filled by invention and innovation. This in turn opened up niches for gas stations, garages, repair shops, and so on; also for tax offices, policemen, courts, highways, cement production, shopping centers, and a great variety of new artifacts. Here again, the heterogeneity of the social environment may preserve shelters for commodities; for instance, the Amish horses and buggies which have become almost extinct in the rest of society. The preservation of these shelters may be important for the perpetuation of the complexity of the human knowledge structure and the long-run history of societal evolution. One sees the same phenomenon with ideas, forms of organizations, types of persons, and other human artifacts.

Mutations in Demand

Mutations also take place in the structure of demand. This may happen because of fashion. There is a certain itch for change in the human race. We get tired of the "same old thing," even if it performs its function satisfactorily. We often see change almost for its own sake. Almost every society has fashion leaders and the changes in their demands—for instance, for clothing, foods, styles of architecture, or even politics—may have a profound effect on the demands of millions of people who look to them as guides. This phenomenon is even more striking in the socialist countries, where the fashions of a very small group of people at the top, in the Politburo or some equivalent organization, may change the demands of millions of people who look to them for guidance. Change in demand can also take place as a result of increased know-how; for instance, when it was discovered that the drug thalidomide had catastrophic effects on the development of infants in the womb, the demand for it completely disappeared. A constant learning process goes on in the operations of buying and selling. We learn often by experience what are the commodities we like or do not like; those that disappoint us we tend not to purchase again, and our demand for them shrinks.

Profit and Interest

A phenomenon in economic systems for which it is hard to find a counterpart in biological systems is that of the rate of profit or the rate of interest. The case of the rate of profit represents essentially a rate of growth of the gross relative value of some stock of commodities organized into a process of production. Thus, an automobile company owns factories, machines, assembly lines, raw materials, land, and stocks of finished automobiles. All these are listed in its balance sheets on the asset side, together with its stock of money and interest-bearing securities. On the liability side we have its debts, its obligations, and its net worth, which is the total value of its assets minus the value of its contractual liabilities. In the course of a year, let us say, automobiles are produced; as they are produced, money is paid out for wages, raw materials, salaries, and other purchases. Plants and machinery are depreciated, their value diminished because of their aging and wear and tear, all of which diminishes net worth. When an automobile is produced it is usually valued at cost until it is sold. Only if it is sold at more than its cost does its production increase the net worth of the business. If a business is successful, the value of sales of its products will exceed what has been sacrificed in net worth and costs, so there will be a net addition to net worth. This is profit. The rate of profit is the rate at which the net worth grows as profits are earned and before they are distributed.

Interest Contracts

Similarly, a rate of interest is the rate of gross growth of the value of a stock of debts or financial instruments, such as bonds or promissory notes. Thus, if the rate of interest is 6 percent per annum, an undisturbed debt (like a savings account) will grow at this rate continually.

Interest is always established by some kind of original contract between the borrower and the lender. The terms of the contract spell out how much will be paid in the first instance by the lender to the borrower and what sums the borrower will repay at specified times in the future. Some of these contracts may be very short term, perhaps only a few days, or months; some like mortgages may go for 20 or even 30 years. For many of these contracts, there is a market in which the contract can be bought and sold, so that the owner of such a contract may not be the original lender, who often sells the contract to somebody else, who may then resell it, and so on. The price at which an interest contract is sold determines the future rate of interest on it for the purchaser, and the rate of interest which the past contract has actually carried for the seller. If A lends B $1000, paid immediately, and B writes a contract to give A $200 on the anniversary of the original contract for each of seven years, and $57 on the eighth year, the rate of interest on this contract, as we see in Table 1, is 10 percent per annum, reckoned annually. If the contract were sold at its 10 percent per annum capital value (line 2, Table 1) at any time (say, for $536 in year four), the seller and the purchaser would both be getting 10 percent on their investment. If it is sold for more than the 10 percent per annum capital value, the seller who made the original loan will be getting more than 10 percent on his investment, and the buyer will be getting less than 10 percent. In general, the higher the price of a given expectation of payments, the less the rate of interest on it. If there is an active market in these contracts, the future rate of interest on them is determined by the price which they fetch in the market. It rises or falls as this price falls or rises.

Several different forms of interest contracts go by somewhat different names: *notes* are rather brief contracts often with a single repayment; *bonds* are contracts which extend for a considerable period of time, often with a constant amount paid every year, sometimes with a larger amount at the end of the contract; *mortgages* are made usually on the

Table 1

Year	0	1	2	3	4	5	6	7	8
Capital	1000	900	790	669	536	390	229	52	0
10% Interest		100	90	79	67	54	39	23	5
Payment		200	200	200	200	200	200	200	57
Repayment of Capital		100	110	121	133	146	161	177	52

security of real estate and tend usually to involve payment of a fixed sum each year until the capital value of the debt falls to zero. The principles involved, however, are the same in all types of interest contracts.

Stocks as Contracts

Stocks are somewhat different. They represent a contract to pay to the owner of the security not fixed amounts at given dates in the future, but variable amounts depending on the profits of the organization. The price of stocks may vary, therefore, not only because the rate of interest itself varies, but also because expectations of the payments made on the stock, or the price of the stock itself, in the future may change, as the prospects of the business improve or decline. Expectations may also affect the price of bonds and interest contracts, where there is uncertainty about whether the contracted payments will actually be made.

Tendencies to Equalizing Profit or Interest Rates

In societies in which there is freedom of ownership and of exchange in securities of various kinds, there is a strong tendency for rates of profit and of interest in different groups and complexes to approach equality, subject to a compensation for nonmonetary factors such as uncertainty, respectability, liquidity, convenience, and so on, which are also relevant to decisions to hold property in one form rather than in another. If all these nonmonetary advantages and disadvantages of various forms of property were equal in all occupations, then if the rate of profit or interest were different for different combinations, there would be a general attempt to buy into those combinations with a high rate and to sell out of those with a low rate. This would raise the price of the combinations with high rates of profit or interest and so lower the rate, and would raise the price of combinations with low rates of profit or interest and so raise the rate, until all the rates came to equality. In fact, of course, the existence of nonmonetary advantages and disadvantages means that forms of property with high nonmonetary advantages will have low monetary advantages—that is, low monetary rates of return, and vice versa. The same phenomenon may be observed in labor markets, where occupations with high monetary advantages or low investment costs tend to have a low money wage compared with occupations with high nonmonetary disadvantages or high investment costs. Again, it is hard to think of a counterpart for this phenomenon in the biological field.

Centrally Planned Chickens Versus Free-Market Ecosystems

Another phenomenon of interest in the economy is the existence of two major "ideal types" of economic systems, neither of which exists in a pure form, but where there is a distinct clustering to one end of the spectrum or the other. One of these types is the centrally planned economy as we find it in the communist countries, in which private property is severely restricted and most productive capital is owned by the state. In this case the survival of a commodity or an occupation or even of types of persons depends on the decisions of the state, operating through the central planning agency, and the social genetic structure (know-how) of the society is concentrated very heavily in a small group of people of great power in the planning office or in the central political organization. At the other end of the scale, we have market-type economies in which private property and free exchange are permitted over large areas of the society, and in which, therefore, the survival of a commodity depends on its ability to satisfy the demand sufficient to ensure a price which will return compensation in real terms to its producers sufficient to persuade them to stay in the occupation and not transfer to some other one.

The centrally planned economy has some parallel to the single biological organism. A chicken is a centrally planned economy derived from the plan in its original fertilized egg. The plan is carried out because of the ability of the genetic structure to direct energy, as we have seen, toward the selection, transportation, and transformation of materials into the form of the phenotype. A market-type economy by contrast is much more like an ecosystem, in which all the various commodities and social products of all kinds interact with each other ecologically and survive if they can find a niche in the total system. Strictly, of course, survival always consists of finding a niche. In the case of the centrally planned economy, however, the niche is very largely determined by the planners, not by the demands of the bulk of the people in the society. This is not to say, of course, that even a centrally planned economy is incapable of organizing itself to respond to the demands of its people, but this response itself depends on the will of the planners, not on the will of the people as individuals, unless the political structure permits the people to replace unacceptable planners.

The Budget as a Plan and the Measure of Failure

All organizations, from the smallest to the largest, involve some degree of central planning, the capitalist corporation just as much as a socialist state. The major instrument of planning is the budget. It is essentially a plan for the allocation of expenditure of money for the purchase of specific kinds of labor and goods. This is the basic genetic structure of the period of the plan—that is, of the budget. The budget, of course, assumes certain know-how and production functions and assumes that doing certain things will produce certain products. And there may, of course, be contingency plans in the budgets if things do not work out as expected. The size of the budget is very strongly related to the money income or inflow of the organization. In the case of the socialist state, this is from sales, from state subsidies ultimately derived from taxes, or from the profits of the state enterprises—that is, the excess of the value of the product over the outlays required to make them. In the case of the capitalist firm or corporation the inflow of money is largely a function of the sales of the product.

The question as to what constitutes a failure is interesting. In the case of the socialist organization, this is the perception of failure to conform to the plan on the part of the planners themselves, who may, of course, be deceived by the people who are supposed to carry out the plan. In the case of the capitalist enterprise failure is measured primarily in the inability to make profits, although this too sometimes is temporarily hidden from the owners by the obfuscation of accounts. Other indicators besides profits also come in, such as public esteem, proneness to government regulation, and so on. Almost all capitalist firms could increase their profits by the sacrifice of a certain sense of prestige and security.

The difference between the chicken and the organization is that the plan of the chicken carries it through growth, into maturity, and eventually to death, whereas the plans of organizations are rarely that long term, and usually run only for a limited period of time after which the plan is revised, often on an annual basis. Socialist countries are rather fond of five-year plans. They are very rarely carried out in full and almost always have to be revised as time goes on. It is a very rare organization that plans at its inception for its own extinction. A few foundations have done this, and the death of an organization, though it not infrequently happens through bankruptcy in the case of the firm, or conquest in the case of the state, is almost always unplanned and comes as an unpleasant surprise.

Dialectics Versus Ecology

The role of dialectical processes in biological and societal evolution is a question of great interest though of considerable difficulty. Dialectical processes can be defined as those which involve struggle, fighting, and conflict among organized systems. This implies some degree of consciousness, in the sense that it represents a form of interaction of large organized systems in which the perception of each system by the other is an important element in the total process. In biological systems dialectical processes as thus defined are of very little importance. What we have, as we have seen, is ecological interaction, most of which is highly unconscious. Almost the only dialectical processes which occur are those involved in the fighting of males and females in sexual selection, and even this frequently leads to extinction rather than to survival of a species. The predator-prey relationship might be interpreted in some sense as a dialectical relationship. Thus, the evolutionary development of protective coloration, speed, elusiveness, and so on, suggests that predator-prey relationships do modify the character and behavior of the species involved. These, however, I would regard as not true dialectical processes simply because for the species the concept of "winning" or "losing" is virtually meaningless. A predator which exterminates its prey will itself become extinct, and the stability of the predator-prey relationship depends on a subtle balance of the skills of the predator and the skills of the prey. Actually the predator-prey relationship is apt to be a very stable one, more stable than mutual cooperation or mutual competition.[3]

In social systems dialectical processes are more significant, and organized conscious struggle has occasionally had important effects on societal evolution. We could ask the question in the form perhaps: How often did it really matter who won a fight? As history is usually written from the point of view of one of the participants in fighting, historians tend to overestimate the significance of these processes. Actually, if we look at the overall evolution of society in knowledge, technology, and culture, we find that these dialectical processes are much less significant than appears at first sight. The ecological processes of invention, discovery, and diffusion explain much more than evolution of human artifacts, or the growth of human populations of different kinds and the great ongoing processes by which the human race moved from the first eolith to the space lab, than do the ups and downs of wars, conquests, revolutions, the rise and fall of empires, political parties, even of religions and classes.

One is tempted to argue that on the whole dialectical processes are the waves and storms on the great streams and tides of human history rather than the streams and tides themselves. Nevertheless, one cannot deny the possibility that at particular times and places it has mattered who won a fight, particularly in what might be called "watershed situations," in which going from one side to the other of an evolutionary watershed may make a great difference in the ultimate result. The overall estimation of the significance of these dialectical processes, however, would involve a very detailed study of the actual historical processes of human evolution and even this would probably not resolve the question. The if's and and's of history are very hard to determine, especially in view of the strong random elements in the processes of human historical development.

Evolution as Lacking Predictive Power

One of the difficulties of evolutionary theory, both in biology and in social systems, is that it does not have very much predictive power. This is inherent in the nature of the process itself and is not simply a remediable defect of human knowledge. Prediction of the future is possible only in systems that have stable parameters like celestial mechanics. The only reason why prediction is so successful in celestial mechanics is that the evolution of the solar system has virtually ground to a halt in what is essentially a dynamic equilibrium with stable parameters. Evolutionary systems, however, by their very nature have unstable parameters. They are disequilibrium systems and in such systems our power of prediction, though not zero, is very limited because of the unpredictability of the parameters themselves. If, of course, it were possible to predict the change in the parameters, then there would be other parameters which were unchanged, but the search for ultimately stable parameters in evolutionary systems is futile, for they probably do not exist.

We do not really know whether the universe is a determinant system or whether it has real randomness in it. This is a question that the human mind can probably never resolve. What is significant for us is that it has epistemological randomness—that is, uncertainty—that beyond a certain point is irreducible. We see this even in physics in the Heisenberg principle—that we cannot "ask" an electron where it is without changing its position. Social systems have Heisenberg principles all over the place, for we cannot predict the future without changing it. Predictions themselves are part of the parameters of the system. What power of prediction we have in evolutionary systems depends on the probability that at least some parameters will not change. The further we look into the future, however, the more the parameters will change and ordinarily the greater the uncertainty.

Convergent Evolution

There is one possible exception to this rule in the case of what might be called "convergent evolution," and there is some evidence for this. We would like to think, for instance, that all evolutionary processes have a high probability of producing intelligence if they go on long enough. On the other hand, as one reflects on the extraordinarily narrow physical limits within which evolution has proceeded on the earth, one realizes that the kind of evolutionary processes which would produce something like the human race may be very rare indeed and always have some probability of being interrupted and stopped. If the earth had been a little bigger or a little smaller, or a little further from the sun, or a little closer to it, or perhaps even if it had not had a moon, or if it had not had the particular combination of elements which it does, then it would have been as sterile of evolution as Venus or Mars. Nevertheless, it is hard not to feel, even though this feeling is something of a leap of faith, that given the kind of physical limits which the earth has had, then the evolution of something like the human race was certainly highly probable.

The "Time's Arrow" of Evolution

We do seem to perceive a "time's arrow" in evolution, certainly toward complexity and control systems, more hesitantly toward awareness, consciousness, and something hard to put a name on that perhaps we dare call intelligence. This may happen because, as we have seen, it is know-how that is the essential element of the processes of production. Energy and materials are limiting factors, but not creative or formative factors. They can limit the realization of know-how and they are necessary to carry and encode the information which is involved in know-how, but evolution fundamentally is a process in genetic material, whether of biological genes or of social know-how, and the phenotypes are just the carriers. Samuel Butler said that "a hen is only an egg's way of making another egg."[4] Biologically, human beings are only gene transmitters. Sociologically, they are more than that because they are self-generators of know-how and value structures. Nevertheless, from the point of view of societal evolution in the large the individual human being is again significant mainly as a knowledge transmitter, however much fun the person may have on the way. If knowledge—that is, the social genetic structure—is not transmitted from one generation to the next, the phenotypes, the artifacts which this knowledge produces, will disappear in a single lifetime. As we become conscious of processes, of course, we change them. The development of the human race, with its capacity for immensely complex images of the world, for images of the future, and for consciousness itself, represents a profound gear change in the whole evolutionary process, as profound indeed as the change which took place with the development of DNA and the beginning of life itself.

One puzzling and rather frightening thing about evolution, whether biological or societal, is that it seems to accelerate in some sense as measured by the intelligence, the complexity, or the amount of know-how which characterizes the state of the system at any one time. Whether this acceleration is an inherent property of the system we do not really know. I do not know of a theoretical model which really produces it, except the one that know-how increases the capacity to know more. Perhaps we can express this by saying that evolution itself evolves, that it is not a single process, but that the process itself constantly changes, and that this leads to acceleration.

Evolutionary Potential

One of the trickiest and yet most important concepts in evolutionary theory is the concept of evolutionary potential. There are some mutations, such as the formation of life itself, for instance, which have in themselves the potential of all that follows. Mutations like the development of sex or the vertebrate skeleton or the central nervous system or the human race itself obviously in hindsight had enormous potential. Evolutionary potential is difficult to define, or to identify, and we do not understand the processes which lead to its generation. We see exactly the same phenomenon in social systems. There are times and places in history in which great evolutionary potential is created—for instance, in the origins of the great religions, the great empires, the great states, the great movements of mankind like science, and so on. We see these potentials, however, only by hindsight. Certainly nobody at the time ever recognizes them. What is even harder to recognize is the potentials that were frustrated, that did not materialize. It is much harder to study and to understand what did not happen than what did. Yet the difficulty is that we cannot really understand what did happen unless we understand why what did not happen did not happen. All this suggests not only that evolution is a pattern which does not endow us with great predictive power but that it is a pattern where even our understanding of the past is very limited and will probably always remain so. Nevertheless, it is all we have, for this is what the world is like, and we must make the best of it.

Economic Development as the Evolution of Commodities

Societal development is a process by which the human race realizes the evolutionary potential for producing artifacts that is inherent in its biologically produced brains. This is the process that goes from the first *Homo* and *Mulier sapiens* with their primitive concepts and artifacts, to Einstein and space shuttles. Economic development is a subset of this process through time and space, now confined to the surface of the earth. It concentrates particularly on the evolution of *commodities*—that is, valued artifacts that at least potentially have the capacity for entering into exchange and transfer. We shall explore this in the next chapter.

Notes

1. Thorstein Veblen, "Why Is Economics Not an Evolutionary Science?" *Quarterly Journal of Economics* XIII (1898): 373.
2. Alfred Marshall, *Principles of Economics* (London: Macmillan, 1st ed., 1890).
3. See Kenneth E. Boulding, *Ecodynamics* (Beverly Hills: Sage Publications, 1978), p. 78.
4. Samuel Butler, *Life and Habit.*

CHAPTER *2*

Commodities as an Evolutionary System

Human History as the Evolution of Artifacts

One thing which differentiates human beings from all other biological species is their capacity to produce an enormous variety and quantity of artifacts. Nonhuman species produce a few artifacts, like the beaver dam and house, birds' nests, gopher holes, termite colonies, and the like, but these are probably done almost entirely by instinct—that is, by genetically produced know-how—and they are highly specialized to each species. Human beings are able to produce an enormous variety and quantity of artifacts because of the capacity of the human nervous system for knowledge and know-how on a very large scale. It is also a consequence of the ability of the human race, both through language and through exchange of commodities, to organize itself into specialized but interacting persons and groups, so that to some extent anything which any one person knows is available to many others through the transmission of knowledge and skills and the exchange of commodities.

The history of the human race is to a large extent the history of the evolution of human artifacts as they have risen in number and complexity. These, we have noted, are of three kinds: material artifacts, organizations, and persons. We can trace the evolution of material artifacts from the first eoliths and flint arrowheads, through crops, metals, houses, cities, and ships to airplanes, computers, Skylab, and space shuttles. We can trace the evolution of organizational artifacts from the early clan, tribe, and family, through the village, the city-state, the empire, the church, the guild to the corporation, the Federal Reserve

System, and the United Nations. We can trace the evolution of persons, insofar as the content of their minds and their skills and behavior is a function of the learning process in society, from the early hunters and gatherers, through the farmers and metal workers, soldiers and emperors, prophets and priests to scientists, spacemen, executives, and presidents. Our particular concern in this chapter is the evolution of those artifacts which can be called economic goods, which either enter into exchange or may potentially enter into exchange, or are valued according to some price or exchange ratio.

Exchange and Reciprocity

We must begin by looking at the phenomenon of exchange itself. Exchange begins very early in human history. There is indeed no known human society which did not possess exchange or at least some kind of reciprocity. It is essential indeed to the operation of a family. The nuclear family in some form, at least consisting of a mother, a father, or surrogates, and children, is also universal, for without it the human race could not, in the past at least, perpetuate itself biologically because of the need of human children for a long period of dependency on adults. Reciprocity probably arises before exchange, and exchange evolves out of it. The distinction between reciprocity and exchange is not wholly clear, as the two phenomena tend to merge into each other. Reciprocity involves a grant of goods or services of some kind from A to B and a corresponding grant, either at the same time or later, from B to A. Exchange likewise involves the transfer of something from A to B and the transfer of something else from B to A. The difference between exchange and reciprocity lies in the degree of explicitness and the contractual arrangement involved. Reciprocal relations are informal, often customary, noncontractual, and often not completely explicit, whereas exchange relations tend to be contractual, formal, and explicit.

Within the family, for instance, we find a great deal of reciprocity—the husband does things for the wife and the wife does things for the husband—but there is very rarely an explicit contractual arrangement to this effect. These transfers are worked out through custom and habit. They are made certainly in the expectation of receiving transfers in return, without, however, a clear prior understanding of what these reciprocal transfers may be. In exchange, by contrast, there is a clear understanding of the terms of the exchange. It begins, for instance, by A communicating with B: "I will give you so much of *x* if you will give me so much of *y*." B may accept the offer, in which case the exchange is then consummated, or may refuse it, or may make a counter offer, which A may then accept. In any case there is a clear understanding before the exchange takes place as to what exactly will be exchanged.

Terms of Trade and of Reciprocity

In both exchange and reciprocity the "terms" are of importance—that is, the ratio of the things exchanged or reciprocated. In exchange, the terms are very clear and are agreed upon beforehand. I may, for instance, see a shirt that I fancy in a store window, with a price tag on it of $15. This price tag is a statement by the owner of the shirt—that is, the storekeeper or the store owner—saying in effect, "I will give this shirt to anybody who gives me $15." If I go into the store and buy the shirt, I have accepted this invitation. The terms of exchange here, or the rate of exchange, as it is often called, is one shirt for $15, which of course is the same thing as two shirts for $30, or three shirts for $45. It is important to understand that the rate of exchange is a ratio, not an absolute number and that, for instance, $.10 per ounce is exactly the same ratio as $1.60 per pound. When one of the things exchanged is money, the ratio of exchange becomes a price. Exchange, however, is a more fundamental concept, and the structure of relative prices is more fundamental than the structure of money prices. Thus, if wheat is $2 a bushel and coffee is $4 a pound, the exchange ratio or relative price of wheat for coffee is one bushel of wheat for one-half pound of coffee, or two bushels of wheat per pound of coffee, meaning that even if we go through the intermediary of money, if we have one bushel of wheat we can transform this through exchange into one-half pound of coffee, and if we have one pound of coffee, we can transform this through exchange into two bushels of wheat.

There are terms of reciprocity as well as terms of exchange; they are less well defined though they may be equally important. We see this even in things like dinner parties or Christmas presents. Someone who does not fairly soon reciprocate an invitation to a dinner party with a return invitation is apt not to be invited next time. An aunt who sends us a Christmas present may stop this practice if she never gets one from us.

The overall terms of trade and reciprocity are of great importance for individuals and for groups. For an individual or a group, the "overall terms" consist of the ratio of what is perceived as being given out to what is perceived as being taken in. If these terms are favorable, it means that a good deal is perceived as taken in for one unit of what is given out. If they are unfavorable, it means that not very much is taken in per unit of what is given out. In formal exchange the terms are very clear: In the wheat market, for instance, the dollar which a buyer gives up is very similar to the dollar which the seller receives, and the wheat which the seller gives up is very similar to the wheat which the buyer receives. The overall terms, however, always involve a strong subjective, perceptual element.

Exchange as Usually Benefiting Both Parties

In free exchange each party has a potential veto—that is, can refuse the contract under the terms proposed by the other. Hence, it has long been a principle of economics that free exchange is believed to be beneficial by both parties at the time a contract is incurred. This does not preclude the possibility that one or the other of the parties may at a later time regret the transaction—that is, may come to think that their belief at the time of the transaction was mistaken and that, if they had known the consequences of the exchange, they would not have entered into it. The purchaser of a car may find out that it is a lemon, though at the time of the purchase this was obviously not known.

There may be deceit in offers to exchange—false advertising, false descriptions, and so on. The buyer or even the seller who is once bitten may be twice shy, so that there is some tendency in society to reduce these deceitful practices to some equilibrium level, the level itself depending on the nature of the information system and the moral and legal pressures which are brought to bear. With this exception, the assertion that exchange benefits both parties is highly defensible. There is, however, a certain paradox in that, while both parties benefit from a well-informed exchange (or it will be vetoed by one or the other), there is a conflict in the rate of exchange if this is variable, as it may be, for instance, in the case of bilateral exchange, where there are no or few alternate exchangers. This is the "bargaining situation" where there is a range of terms of exchange within which both parties are willing to consummate the transaction, but where also the division of the gain depends on the price which was actually reached. The higher the price, the more of the total gain from trade goes to the seller and the less to the buyer; the lower the price, the more goes to the buyer and the less to the seller.

Elements of Reciprocity in Exchange

The terms of reciprocity are vaguer, but extremely important psychologically. In a marriage, for instance, if one partner feels that he or she is giving a great deal and not getting very much, the continuation of the marriage may be in question. Divorce occurs indeed precisely at the point where one party feels that the overall terms of the relationship are so low that it is not worth continuing and that some alternative situation offers better terms. One problem here is that because of the highly subjective nature of reciprocity, the terms may be perceived very differently by the two parties. In exchange, there is a fairly objective price or ratio of exchange, and the movement of this, as we can see, redistributes the benefit of exchange between the parties. In reciprocity, however, it is quite possible for both parties at the same time to feel that their terms of reciprocity have either worsened or improved, for what one party perceives as giving up is not necessarily at all what the other perceives as receiving. A may give B flowers as an expression of love and B may interpret the flowers as an insult.

The Labor Market

Many transactions are mixtures of exchange and reciprocity. A good example are the transactions in the labor market, where there is an exchange of hours of work for money, but where also there are strong elements of reciprocity in actual activity undertaken. The environment and conditions of work, the sense of dependence or independence, the congeniality, or otherwise, of workmates and supervisors, the sense of risks being taken, the chances of promotion or the fear of being in a dead end are all elements in the labor bargain which are rarely spelled out in the contract. The reciprocal elements in the labor transaction are reflected in the fact, again, that what one party receives is not the same thing that the other party gives up. Thus, when an employer hires a worker for wages what the employer gives up is the money wage and really consists in the alternative uses of the money, so that if he employs the worker, he gives up a secure, but perhaps not very productive use of the money in a savings account for a risky, but perhaps more productive use of the money in a productive enterprise. What the worker receives is not so much the money as the purchasing power of the money—that is, what it will buy in the stores or in other markets. Similarly, what the worker gives up is the alternative uses of his or her time, either for leisure, for other employment, or for self-employment. What the employer receives is the value of the product of the work, or rather the anticipation of this value which may or may not be realized either in terms of the product or of its value. It is not surprising that the labor contract is beset by so many sociological difficulties and that it produces a very different social situation from, for instance, exchanges in the stock market or the foreign exchange market, or even the organized commodity markets, where on the whole what the buyer gives up is very much what the seller receives, and what the seller gives up is very much the same thing as the buyer receives, and where the buyer and seller essentially belong to the same subculture.

Terms as Behavioral Reinforcers

The overall terms of trade and reciprocity are of great importance in positive or negative reinforcement of previous behavior. If the overall terms are perceived to be poor by either party, there will be less incentive to indulge in similar exchanges or relationships in the future, and alternatives will be sought, either by trying to find new parties to the exchange or by trying to find or produce new things to exchange. After the introduction of the automobile, horse breeders found that their overall terms of exchange and reciprocity were falling. They could not sell the number of horses they previously had been doing, so if they stayed in horse breeding, they would have to lower the relative prices of horses in terms of other things, and they would feel themselves becoming worse off. Two possible reactions to this would be, first, looking for other markets as, for instance, riding stables, or horses for pleasure, or, second, abandoning the occupation altogether and turning, say, to cattle feeding or industrial occupations, which promised a better return. On the other hand, people who find their overall terms of exchange and reciprocity favorable are apt to continue and expand what they have previously been doing and increase the output of their product.

Commodities as an Ecosystem
with Ecological Equilibrium

We now look at the world of commodities as if it were an ecosystem. Each commodity is a species. At any one moment it has a population or stock. There is, for instance, at any one moment in a society a population of automobiles as there is a population of humans or of rabbits. This stock, as we have seen, is added to by production, which corresponds to birth in the case of biological species, or by imports (inmigration) and subtracted from by consumption, which corresponds to death in biological species, or by exports (outmigration). Just as in biological species, species of human artifacts consist of individuals of different ages and therefore of different age-related characteristics. One difference between biological and social species is that individuals in biological species tend to be born in an immature condition and have to grow into maturity, after which they decline into old age if they do not die first. Social species tend to be born—that is, emerge from the factory or the workshop—in an almost completely mature condition and they begin to age immediately. It is certainly not farfetched, however, to consider the immature automobile on the assembly line as a fetus, and the difference in life pattern of social and biological species, while significant for some purposes, is not really fundamental.

The greatest difference between social and biological species, as we have already observed, is that biological species carry their own genetic instructions within the phenotype, but the social species do not. This separation of the phenotype from the genetic instructions which initiated and guided its production can give societal evolution some very different characteristics from biological evolution.

The critical question in both cases, and indeed for the total ecosystem of social and biological species taken together, is whether there is some set of stocks or population totals for each species at which the additions to its stock through births or production is equal to the subtractions from its stock through deaths or consumptions, and hence the stock (population) tends to remain stable. We neglect migration in this model. Ecologists postulate, for instance, climactic ecosystems in the biosphere in which the population of each species has risen to its "niche" and is relatively stable, with perhaps some fluctuations. The concept of long-run equilibrium of the commodity system of Alfred Marshall is very similar to that of a climactic ecosystem. It postulates that, with a given knowledge and technology structure (corresponding to a given genetic composition of the ecosystem), populations of commodities will expand or contract until for each of them production equals consumption and the population is relatively stable. This equilibrium will be stable if an increase (from equilibrium) in the population of any species results in an excess of deaths over births, so that the population falls back to the equilibrium level, or if a decrease in population results in an excess of births over deaths, so that the population rises to the equilibrium level. These are very plausible assumptions.

Ecological Interaction Through the Relative Price Structure

In the case of commodity species the ecological interaction is mediated mainly through the relative price structure. As we have seen, the relative price structure helps to determine the perceived overall terms of trade and reciprocity of the persons concerned with production and consumption of these commodities. We can suppose that there is some "equilibrium" structure of relative prices, which creates a structure of overall returns or perceived terms of trade and reciprocity, such that nobody feels on balance that he or she can improve his or her position by changing from the production of one commodity to the production of another. I say "on balance" because this does not preclude shifts of persons from one occupation to another, provided these shifts all offset each other—that is, provided that the number of people (and their resources) coming into an occupation are equal to the number going out.

It must be emphasized that the concept of an equilibrium relative price structure, like that of a climactic ecosystem, is an intellectual construct, that such things are never found in exact form in the real world, though there may be approximations to them, for the real world is a system under evolution—that is, under constant change. Nevertheless, it is a useful intellectual construct. It gives us, as it were, a halfway house to the understanding of the total dynamics of the system. The question of the stability of the possible equilibrium of these systems is important, for unless the real world has a tendency toward equilibrium over time there is not much point in postulating a theoretical equilibrium, as it would not throw any real light on the overall dynamic system. Systems in unstable equilibrium tend not to be around and are seldom observed! In the case of the equilibrium of the ecosystem of commodities, two steps may be postulated: The first is that with a given structure of preferences the relative price structure in the market itself—that is, in the actual exchanges which are taking place in a brief period of time—is a function of the total stocks of all commodities, including money and financial assets of various kinds. The existence of services—that is, of commodities with a very short life, like hearing an opera—present some difficulties. Even commodities with a zero length of life, which are virtually unknown, could be perceived just as limiting cases. An opera could be thought of as producing a psychological commodity—"Just having gone to the opera"—which exists as a stock among the human population and which in each individual case depreciates to the point where, if we are opera fans, we have to go to another opera to refurbish it. The distinction between goods and services, therefore, is not really fundamental and for present purposes can be neglected.

Equilibrium Sets of Market Prices and Normal Prices

We can then suppose that with any given structure of preferences, or each set of total stocks of commodities, there is some relative price structure—that is, set of prices—at which the holders of commodities on balance are willing to hold what is there to be held. This might be called the "market equilibrium price set." If the actual prices in actual exchanges on any one day, shall we say, are different from the equilbrium market price set, some prices will be above the equilibrium, some will be below, and some may be equal to it. For those commodities where the price is above the equilibrium and is therefore perceived in some sense in the aggregate as "too high," there will be a net attempt to unload the commodity; that is, there will be an excess of offers to sell over offers to buy. There will be unsatisfied sellers who will tend to lower the price at which they are offering to sell, so the prices that are "too high" will tend to fall. Similarly, prices that are "too low" will produce a situation in which there is a net attempt to acquire the commodity, there will be an excess of offers to buy over offers to sell, there will be unsatisfied buyers, and some of these unsatisfied buyers will raise the price at which they are offering to buy. Or if sellers set the price, they will realize that they will be able to raise prices and still find buyers, so the sellers will raise the prices. Who actually sets the price, whether the buyers or the sellers, or even whether the price is set by some bargaining between them, is important to some problems, but it is not particularly important in this simple model.

Thus, corresponding to any given set of stocks of commodities there is an equilibrium set of market prices toward which the existing market price will tend to move. If this movement is very slow, cyclical processes may be set up which might destroy the stability of the equilibrium, but for the moment we will neglect these. We can now go on to postulate a long-run equilibrium set of "normal" prices at which the production and consumption of each commodity is equal and the stock does not change. If the set of market prices does not correspond to this, some prices, again, will be "too high" and some will be "too low." For a commodity whose price is "too high," production will be encouraged and consumption will be discouraged, and the total stock or population of the commodity will tend to rise. As it rises, however, the equilibrium market price tends to fall, as we have seen, and this will bring about a fall in the actual market price relative to others. This fall will diminish production and expand consumption and will go on to the point at which production and consumption are equal.

Conditions can be postulated in which these equilibria are not stable. These conditions, however, are a little unlikely and the record of experience suggests that relatively stable equilibrium ranges of both prices, stocks, production, and consumption of commodities, as well as births and deaths of biological species, are extremely common. For instance, disturb a pond by taking a proportion of a certain fish out of it and in a year or two the old quantities are back again. The depleted fish population expands into its old niche. Similarly, in social systems we disturb the ecosystem, for instance, by the prohibition of the production of alcoholic beverages. Once that prohibition is removed, the alcoholic beverage industry grows back to a size not unlike what it was before. A war disturbs the demand for commodities and results in an increased production of weapons and an expansion of the armed forces. Once the war is over, the pattern of production and of prices returns to something like—though never quite like—what it was before the war.

Alternative Costs

An important property of all ecosystems which is of particular significance in the ecosystem of economic goods is the structure of alternative costs. The most general concept of alternative costs is what amount has to be given up in terms of some characteristic of one species A if there is a unit increase in this characteristic in species B. The characteristic can be population itself, in which case we think of alternative costs as the diminution of the population of species A which results from a unit increase in the population of species B. If an increase of one wolf in the wolf population produces a diminution of eight rabbits in the rabbit population, the alternative cost is eight rabbits per wolf. In economic systems, it is frequently the throughput of the population—that is, its births and deaths or production and consumption—which is regarded as more significant. The alternative cost here would be the decline in the rate of production of one commodity which resulted from a unit increase in the rate of production of another.

Alternative costs arise because of scarcity—that is, because there are some limitations in the system of know-how, energy, or materials, which means that in an ecological equilibrium at least we certainly cannot have indefinitely large quantities of anything. Scarcity means, therefore, that if we have more of one thing we must have less of something else. In Adam Smith's famous example of deer and beaver,[1] labor is treated as a limiting factor that creates the scarcity—that is, it is supposed that there are only so many person-hours of activity possible per day in a given tribe. Then, if it takes one day's labor to catch a deer and two days to catch a beaver, this means that if we give up one beaver (that is, reduce the beaver catch by one) with the labor released we can get two deer (that is, increase the deer catch by two), production here being considered the significant variable. We cannot increase the deer production without giving up some beaver production because of the underlying principle of scarcity, reflected in the fact that the alternative cost is two deer per beaver.

The concept of alternative cost is quite independent of what we regard as the source of the scarcity. It does not depend in any way on the assumption that labor is the source of the scarcity. It could just as well be space, time, energy, materials, or some very complex function combining a number of different elements. There may well be one limitation which is dominant in a particular situation and hence determines the degree of scarcity in the alternative cost structure. It may, for instance, be energy, water, space, the structure of habitats, and so on. As the scarcity imposed by one limitation diminishes, another limitation may take over. Thus, in the Arctic tundra it is almost certainly the scarcity of solar energy which is the major limiting factor. There is usually plenty of water, carbon dioxide, minerals, and so on. In the desert solar energy may be extremely plentiful, but the scarcity of water limits the populations. It could even be that under certain circumstances scarcity of certain trace elements would be the major factor producing alternative costs.

Alternative Costs in Biological Systems

Alternative costs are not a particularly noticeable property of biological ecosystems until there is some mutation, and then the effect of the mutation depends on the structure of alternative costs. Thus, suppose there were a genetic mutation in wolves which increases their hunting capacity. The equilibrium population of wolves may increase and that of rabbits may diminish. If the alternative cost is one wolf per eight rabbits, then if the wolf population increases by ten, the rabbit population will diminish by eighty. On the famous principle that you cannot ever do only one thing or even two things, this change will ramify through the whole ecosystem. Other prey animals will also diminish and other predators may also diminish because of the competition of the wolves. Some things, of course, might increase as the result of the favorable mutation in wolves; for instance, if wolves have any specialized parasites, or if their droppings are favorable to a certain type of plant. Secondary effects like this, again, will ramify all through the system. And when they are all worked out, we ought to be able to specify the alternative costs of the increase in one wolf to all the species in the ecosystem. It is possible, of course, for this alternative cost to be so high for some species that they will actually disappear and become extinct, and that, again, would ramify all through the ecosystem.

It is a very interesting question as to whether a single set of alternative costs can be postulated in a particular ecosystem or whether there is a set which is characteristic of each species. The former situation could only possibly be obtained if all species were mutually competitive with each other, which is virtually unknown. And even there it is by no means certain that the effects would be reciprocal. That is, if an increase in A of one unit produced a decline in B of x units, would an increase in B of x units produce a decline in A of one unit? Where we have predation, it is clear that each species has its own set of alternative costs. An increase in one wolf may diminish the rabbit population by eight, but if there is a mutation which improves the position of rabbits, an increase in rabbits is likely to produce an increase in wolves rather than a diminution, so that the alternative cost is actually negative. Where two species A and B are mutually cooperative, a favorable mutation in one will increase the population of the other. The alternative costs, again, are negative (an increase in A increases B), though there will of course be positive alternative costs somewhere else in the system.

Alternative Costs in Economic Systems; Effects of Mutation on Output

The structures of alternative cost are of great importance in economic systems and they differ, as might be expected, from what are in many ways the simpler ecosystems of biology. We have to ask ourselves, "What do we mean by a favorable mutation in the case of a commodity?" A favorable mutation in the case of Commodity X is clearly some change which will increase its role in the total system relative to other commodities. This may mean either an increase in its total production or consumption or an increase in its overall stock or population. These two things frequently but not necessarily go together. Economic systems differ from biosystems in that the niche of a commodity is determined mainly by the demand for it—that is, the willingness of people to purchase it. Changes in demand then represent mutations in the system. A commodity's place in the system, however, is also determined to some extent by its conditions of supply, which are reflected in its alternative cost—that is, if production of one commodity is expanded, how much must the production of other commodities be diminished because of the principle of scarcity? Favorable mutation here would represent an improvement in the methods of production which would take less of whatever it is that creates the scarcity in order to produce a single unit of the commodity.

Let us take as an example a single commodity—say, coffee. Suppose there is a large increase in the number of Mormons and Seventh-Day Adventists who do not drink it, or let us suppose that somebody discovered that it is carcinogenic, so that large numbers of people become afraid of it and give it up. This represents a fall in the demand for coffee. From the point of view of coffee it is clearly an unfavorable mutation. The first impact would be large unsaleable stocks of coffee, which would sharply reduce the price. As the price falls, coffee production would become extremely unprofitable, coffee producers would go out of business, coffee plantations would be turned over to other things, and every year the production of coffee would decline. Eventually it would decline to the point where there were no longer surplus stocks, the price would rise, coffee production would again become normally profitable but at a very much lower level of output, and also of stocks. If, on the other hand, the medical profession suddenly found that drinking coffee was very good for you, there would be an increase in demand, the price would rise sharply, coffee production would become extremely profitable, production would increase, and the price would eventually come down again to the point where production was about normally profitable. This would clearly be with an increased output, which would clearly be a favorable mutation from the point of view of coffee.

Now let us suppose there is a marked technical improvement in the production of coffee, so that at a lower price it is just as profitable to produce as it was before. At the existing price there will be an expansion of production; this will lead to a fall in price but still at an expanded output. This, again, from the point of view of coffee, is clearly a favorable mutation. Now let us suppose there is a worldwide disease of coffee plants, or a worldwide adverse change in climate which reduces the areas suitable for growing coffee. This would be an unfavorable mutation, the output of coffee would decline, and the price would rise, again to the point where it was normally profitable. We are assuming here that there is no monopolistic intervention.

Effects on Price Structure

In the case of a single commodity, various favorable and unfavorable mutations are likely to produce some changes in the general structure of relative prices, though these changes are likely to be much smaller than the changes in relative outputs. To go back to the case of coffee, if there is a sharp decline in demand, we will end up with a much smaller output of coffee, but this is likely to be concentrated in the most favorable places, where costs of production are lower than in the plantations that have been abandoned. There is some relative price of coffee then which will give normal returns to the producers, which will be a little lower than it had been before, assuming no technical change in the coffee industry.

If variations in the output of a commodity do not result in much change in its alternative costs, and therefore in the relative price at which the production is normally profitable, changes in demand will not produce much change in the price structure. In economists' language the long-run supply is then said to be elastic. There are cases, however, where long-run supply may be inelastic and the output is incapable of much expansion even under the stimulus of higher prices, as further additions to output can be obtained only at sharply increasing alternative costs. A classic example is, of course, rare paintings by dead painters, which cannot be increased at all, and where, therefore, an increase in demand is likely to result in a sharp rise in price, the supply being perfectly inelastic. Some uses of land also fall in this category. Land in Manhattan is extremely high priced because of the high demand; and land in the Adirondacks, which is very cheap, cannot come to New York City in response to this high price which may be a million times the price in the Adirondacks, whereas if wages in New York were even five times what they are in the Adirondacks there would be a flood of population into New York, which would soon reduce the wages, the supply of labor in New York being elastic through migration.

Monopoly Power and the Competitive Model

The mechanism outlined in the last few pages may be modified, though not fundamentally destroyed, by the existence of monopoly power and what the economist calls "imperfections in the market." Economists have postulated a condition called "perfect competition" in which there are so many buyers and sellers interacting in the market that the impact of any one of them is negligible. Any particular buyer or seller can then buy or sell as much as is wanted at the price going in the market, without these particular sales or purchases noticeably affecting the market price itself. Buyers and sellers under this condition do not have to take account of any effect of their own purchases or sales on the price itself. Competition in production implies that anyone who believes that with a given structure of prices they will be better off in another occupation, producing another commodity, would be free to make the switch without being subject to anyone else's veto and at a cost which is small in relation to the potential benefits from the change. The conditions are never found in an extreme form in practice, although they are frequently approximated. We also not infrequently get conditions which are quite widely different from the postulates of perfect competition.

Perfect Monopoly

The furthest extreme is "perfect monopoly," in which a single buyer, seller, or producer can prevent anyone else from entering the market or from producing the product. There are cases close to this in the "natural monopolies"—for instance, in a single electric power company in a given locality—but these are almost always subject to political regulation. In practice monopoly power is nearly always limited in some degree also by the existence of actual or potential substitutes for a product or the development of potential competitors. Attempts to create monopoly power by means of cartels, commodity agreements, and so on have rarely been successful for very long in the absence of some kind of state intervention to repress competition, simply because a monopoly price, by making a particular occupation unusually attractive, will encourage the production of substitutes or even new producers of the commodity in question in other parts of the world, and it is usually very hard to prevent this.

OPEC

A possible exception to this principle, and an example of the successful exercise of monopoly power, is OPEC. There are relatively few oil exporters, and the core of them, namely the Arab countries, are united by common political objectives. Furthermore, at the moment there are no good substitutes for the product and a constantly rising demand. It is not surprising, therefore, that monopoly power is being exercised and that the oil users have to pay what is in effect a tax or tribute to the oil producers. Even here, given 25 years, one suspects that monopoly price will produce substitutes and increase production outside of OPEC, which may eventually undermine its power. Organizational monopoly power always rests on the creation of contrived inelasticities of supply not depending on underlying physical conditions. These organizational structures may turn out to be fragile, particularly in the absence of government control of potential competitors.

Monopoly in the Social Ecosystem

Even monopoly, however, does not destroy the ecological system of commodities and prices outlined above; it merely modifies it in the direction of "artificial" diminution of the niche of the monopolized commodity with a corresponding increase in the economic welfare of its occupants. If one were to look for a biological parallel, one would find it perhaps in territoriality of birds like the robins, which ensures that the total number of robins in the total ecological niche is less than it would be without it, and that therefore the individual robins are more prosperous and have an easier time of it than they would if population were limited by inputs like food. It is rare indeed to see an unprosperous-looking robin. The prosperity of the Arabs may be a somewhat similar phenomenon. In particular, it is not true that the ecological mechanism outlined above stands or falls by the assumption of perfect competition, which is virtually nonexistent in the real world and only would represent an extreme case of the system. Perfect competition has a certain parallel to populations in biological ecosystems which are limited only by the food supply, perhaps the most extreme form of ecological competition. This is rare, and ecological theory in no way depends on this assumption.

Selection and Mutation in the Economy

It must be recognized, however, that both biological systems and social and economic systems are not only ecological systems exhibiting what might be called at least "quasi-equilibrium properties," but are also evolutionary systems. Evolution I defined earlier as ecological interaction under conditions of constantly changing parameters. The change in parameters is mutation; ecological interaction is selection. Mutation can take the form, for instance, of climatic or geological change, ice ages, volcanic eruptions, changes in the composition of the atmosphere or the ocean, droughts, and so on. These, however, we tend to regard as limiting conditions of the system, and we see evolution both biological and societal as primarily a process in the genetic structure—that is, in the structure of information or know-how which constitutes the potential for the production of the "phenotypes," or products, both biological (for instance, a chicken) or social (for instance, an automobile, a corporation, or a computer programmer). To me it is a somewhat awesome thought that a simple safety pin is a product of four billion years of mutation and selection in this part of the universe.

In biological systems, as we have seen, the essential change is in the genetic structure and it is the unending selection of mutations in the genetic structure which constitute the drive of evolution toward ever-increasing complexity. Selection takes place mainly in the phenotypes—that is, mutation is in the egg; selection is in the chicken. Social mutation is not dissimilar. It also has a genetic structure in the form of human know-how and its prosthetic devices in the shape of libraries, blueprints, computers, laboratories, and so on. This know-how, again, is able to direct energy, to sustain temperatures, and to select, transport, and transform chemical elements into improbable structures, not only of skin, blood, and brains, but of walls, water pipes, and computers.

Here again, mutation is primarily in the genetic structure of the know-how—new ideas, new skills, new knowledge. Selection again is in the phenotype. If a mutation in knowledge, a new idea, produces a commodity for which there is no demand at a price which will make it worthwhile producing, that commodity will not be produced, or, if it is produced, it will soon disappear. There will be surplus stocks of it, and these will force the price down to the point where it no longer pays to produce it. An unsuccessful mutation in the genetic structure, whether social or biological, is one which will not be able to produce a phenotype that has a niche in the total ecosystem. New and successful phenotypes, on the other hand, will change the ecosystem and will change the niches of all the old species. Some of these niches may be reduced to zero, in which case the species becomes extinct. This process of the creation of new species through genetic mutation and the extinction of old species through the diminution of niches has been going on now for two or three billion years. It finally produced the human race and the human race in turn has produced enormous quantities of artifacts, all following the same general principle.

Economic Development as the Evolution of Human Artifacts

What we call "economic development" is a process essentially in the evolution of human artifacts—that is, in the development first of all of new know-how in the human population, and in the second place, know-how which has the capacity for producing artifacts which have a niche in the total ecosystem. Again, the production of new artifacts may or may not make old artifacts obsolete and move them toward extinction. It seems much rarer for human than for biological artifacts actually to become extinct and for the genetic knowledge component which underlies them to disappear. Human knowledge is remarkably capable of storage, much more so than the knowledge involved in the biological genetic system. Once a biological species becomes extinct, that is the end of it. There is no known example, I believe, of a biological species that has been revived once it has become extinct, because the genetic know-how is stored in the phenotype itself, and when that is gone, the genetic know-how is likewise gone. The genetic structure—that is, the know-how—of social systems, however, can be stored in innumerable different social species. It is as if, for instance, the genes of the dinosaur could be found in the tissues of the elephants. Furthermore, the human organism has an extraordinary capacity for creating know-how. Thus, the discovery of the Rosetta Stone in Egypt enabled Egyptologists to reconstruct the lost language of the hieroglyphs, and so to revive a "social gene" that had become extinct. We have now been able to reproduce among anthropologists the skills of the old makers of flint knives and arrowheads which had been lost perhaps for thousands of years. Given an artifact which has survived, the human mind has a strong probability of being able to find out how to make it.

Are Mutations Random?

A very interesting question in the history of human development is the extent to which mutations, in the form of new ideas, inventions, and so on have been the result of random and accidental events and the extent to which they are guided by the existence of "empty niches" in the ecosystem of commodities. This is a question which is almost impossible to answer in any exact way. It seems not unreasonable to suppose that there are two sources of inventions, necessity on the one hand and curiosity on the other. Richard G. Wilkinson in *Poverty and Progress*[2] argues that particularly in the earlier periods of economic development, beginning, say, with the transition into the neolithic, population pressures played an important role. With a given technology the human race has a strong tendency to expand into the niche which is appropriate to that technology. We then, however, run into the famous Malthusian principle, that if the only thing that can check the growth of human population is misery in some form, whether this is actual food shortage or whether it is the intensification of conflict or some kind of psychological disorder (and there can be many sources of misery), then the population will expand until it is sufficiently miserable for the expansion to cease.

Development as Niche Expansion: Necessity and Invention

The human being, however, is intensely ingenious, and faced with misery tries to get out of it. This is where necessity becomes the mother of invention. It may be, for instance, that as the advancing ice of the last ice age forced paleolithic humans into increasingly congested and harsher environments they began to look around for other means of subsistence and so perhaps in two or three different places independently discovered agriculture. With the discovery of agriculture, the human niche expanded very largely, perhaps to ten or even a hundred times what it had been in the earlier hunting-and-gathering societies. Then the human race proceeded to fill—or overfill—this new niche, as the teeming villages of Asia, the crowded fields of Europe, and even perhaps the abandoned pueblos of the American Southwest testify.

On another level it may well have been the denudation of the forests with the rise in the agricultural populations and subsequent scarcity of wood which led to the development of metals and the rise of civilization. As an old commodity becomes scarce and hence expensive, its price rises and payoffs for finding substitutes increase, and it is not surprising if the search for mutation—that is, for new ideas, skills, and technologies—is directed toward those things which are potential substitutes for those commodities which become scarcer and rise in price.

Whether there is anything corresponding to this phenomenon in biological systems, we really do not know. Certainly biological mutation, as far as we know, does not involve any conscious images of the future. On the other hand, if the rate of mutation is large enough, the probability is very high that a mutation will occur which produces a phenotype that can fill an empty niche. Hence, evolution may be directed much more by the existence of potential niches than by the actual forms of mutation. Nevertheless, the potentialities of mutation, even in biological evolution, must be important. It is clear that mutation from any given genetic structure is not random in the sense that all mutations are equally probable. Some mutations may be much more probable than others. On the other hand, an improbable mutation which produces a successful species will eventually occur if we wait long enough and if the niche remains empty.

Evolution as Indeterminate

One reason why evolution is so unpredictable is that it is governed by essentially improbable events. Whether, for instance, an improbable mutation will occur during the existence of some empty niche and so fill the niche and change the course of evolution, or whether it will occur only after mutations elsewhere have done away with this niche and so be still-born and leave the course of evolution unchanged, is in the hands of the celestial dice. Evolution is not a determinate system like celestial mechanics because it is not an equilibrium system. It involves an inherently unpredictable change of parameters because of the long-run importance of improbable events. It is a solemn thought that in the twenty billion years of the history of the universe an event with an annual probability of one in two billion has almost certainly happened. One sometimes wonders if this perhaps was not us. Certainly the evolution of the human brain by ordinary processes of natural selection seems extremely improbable in view of the fact that it is such a redundant organ.

Energy and Materials as Limiting Factors; the "Goldilocks Principle"

We must now look at the limits imposed on evolutionary processes by possible scarcities of energy and materials. Energy and materials are necessary for evolution even though they are limiting factors rather than determining factors, for evolution, again, is a process essentially in knowledge or know-how, coded in some kind of information structure. Information, however, has to be coded in some structure of energy or materials, though the same information can be coded in many different structures. Thus, the English sentence which I am composing begins as a structure in my brain; this is coded into a structure of speech muscles, then of air waves as I dictate; the air waves are coded into an electronic structure in the dictaphone, which in turn is coded into a magnetic structure in the tape; the tape is retranslated into air waves, into neural patterns in my secretary's brain, into patterns in her hands, and into typewriter letters on a paper, which in turn may be read, retranslated into the neural patterns of the reader, and retranslated into air waves if it is read aloud. In all this recoding the message retains almost exactly the same structure of information, and in each case it required either a structure of energy impulses or a structure of material patterns in order to encode it.

Evolution, therefore, can only take place in the presence of appropriate forms of energy and appropriate forms of materials capable of complex coding and transmission of information. It did not take place on the moon beyond the evolution of the crystal because of the absence of crucial materials, such as water, though the moon has all the energy from the sun that the earth does. It does not seem to have taken place on Mars, perhaps because of a deficiency in energy and inadequate temperatures, though at one time in the evolution of the planet there does seem to have been water. Earth, like the Little Bear's porridge (I have sometimes called this the "Goldilocks principle") was "just right," with the right amount of energy from the sun and the right materials in the shape of water, with an atmosphere consisting of carbon dioxide and oxygen, and plenty of carbon (which is the great building block of organic complexity, with its small size and its quadrivalent capabilities for hitching onto other atoms). The information in the DNA molecule, which is enormous, is coded in a double helix of carbon atoms with attached carbon, oxygen, hydrogen, and nitrogen atoms. There are also certain trace elements which seem to be necessary for certain life processes.

In economic development, also, the limitations imposed by the scarcities of energy or materials have frequently been significant. Energy and materials will not in themselves create economic development, which is a process essentially inside the "noosphere" (the collective heads of humankind), but the absence of energy and materials in certain forms can limit it. We see this most clearly perhaps in the extremely severe and adverse environments—for instance, of the Arctic, where the Eskimos, a people of extraordinary ingenuity and capability, were able to adapt to the severe environment and to survive in it. Because of the scarcity of solar energy and of soil, however, they could not develop agriculture, hence were not able to develop food surpluses, and had to devote most of their energy to food production. Thus, they were not able to develop cities or anything we could call "civilization," even though their artistic life is rich and they may well be superior to many other groups of humans in intellectual capacity.

For agriculture to develop, there had to be sufficient water and sufficient soil, as well as wild plants which could be domesticated and improved. The domestication of livestock likewise depended on the pre-existence of wild species. The fact, for instance, that the horse disappeared in North America shortly after the invasion of the ancestors of the American Indian about 11,000 B.C.—almost certainly because it was eaten to extinction—meant that the subsequent civilizations of the Aztecs and Incas could not domesticate the horse because there were no horses to domesticate, though they did domesticate the alpaca and the llama. Similarly, in places where there are no mines—that is, no concentrated deposits of metals or metal ore—it is impossible to develop metallurgical techniques, as is the case for the most part in Polynesia, again in spite of the great intelligence and ingenuity of the people.

Energy in Evolution

The role of energy in human evolution, even perhaps in biological evolution, is extraordinarily important and not wholly understood. It looks as if each new expansion of the human niche has been strongly associated with the discovery of new sources of energy, which have pushed back the energy limitation on productive processes. This was true, for instance, of the invention of agriculture, which is a more efficient way of using solar energy in the production of food than is food gathering. A rice paddy, for instance, can produce perhaps a hundred times, perhaps a thousand times as much food as the forest which preceded it, simply because rice is a much more efficient converter of solar energy into carbohydrates and protein than are trees. The development of metals may have depended on the ability to use up existing stocks of wood and frequently resulted in the denudation of forests and economic decline, as we find in what is now Turkey and Greece, and indeed as happened in England in the seventeenth century when the iron industry was threatened by deforestation. The forests were the first "fossil fuel," representing as they do fossil sunshine—that is, the solar energy captured by the photosynthesis of earlier years. Many societies have risen and fallen as they first learned how to exploit these stocks of energy in the forest and then use them up, and eventually had to fall back on the current income of solar energy, often in a very depleted environment.

The discovery of what we more ordinarily think of as fossil fuels—that is, coal, oil, and natural gas—represented another enormous expansion of the energy inputs into human societies and temporarily at least expanded the human niche to the point where we find it today. The growth of the whole temperate zone in economic production in the last hundred years is very closely connected with the discovery of oil and natural gas in 1859, in Titusville, Pennsylvania. That year the human race discovered an enormous treasure chest and we have been doing what everybody does who discovers a treasure chest—we have been living it up, spending our treasure with great enjoyment. In a relatively short time this particular treasure chest will be empty and either we will have to find new treasure chests—that is, new energy stocks—perhaps in uranium, thorium, and eventually deuterium, or we will have to fall back on our energy income from the sun, and this may be quite painful. Until now at any rate most societies which relied almost wholly on solar energy and were not able to use energy stocks have rarely achieved much more than general misery in regard to the level of income. This does not rule out the possibility, however, of a greatly improved technology and the utilization of the energy income from the sun, though this technology still seems to lie in the future.

The materials limitation seems less fundamental than the energy limitation, simply because if we have energy we can at least theoretically recycle materials. There is a constant tendency, furthermore, as existing materials used in the economy become scarcer and more expensive, to substitute the then cheaper and more plentiful materials and to develop a technology for their use. A good example would be the replacement of copper by glass and laser beams in the transmission of electrical energy. We cannot rule out the possibility, however, that rising shortages of materials might limit economic growth in the future, though they have certainly not been a significant factor in the last 100 or 200 years. Furthermore, the recycling of materials may run into sharp limits as human activity constantly makes materials more diffuse and less concentrated, and hence requires more energy to do recycling, which always involves concentrating the diffuse.

Exhaustion Versus Replenishment

We can see economic development, indeed, as the result of two processes which go in opposite directions: One is the exhaustion of known stocks of energy and materials; the other we might call "replenishment," the constant growth of knowledge and discovery. The growth of knowledge, and therefore replenishment, in turn may be influenced by two opposing tendencies: one, the tendency for an increase in knowledge to increase knowledge about how to get more knowledge; the second, the tendency for exhaustion of knowledge potential as we find out all there is to know about certain areas. Geography is a good example: Our knowledge of the crude geography of the earth is now virtually complete, which it was not even when I was a student, when there were still white spaces on the map of the world where today there are none. On the other hand, the accurate mapping of the world has permitted a substantial increase in the knowledge about its inner structure and geology and about human geography and the spatial structure of social systems.

The exhaustion principle means that of known stocks of energy and materials we are likely to use the cheapest and most convenient first, so that as time goes on we use up the cheapest sources and have to go to more expensive ones, and the relative price of both energy and materials continually rises. If knowledge were constant the exhaustion principle would dominate. In the last 200 years replenishment due to the rise of knowledge has far more than offset these exhaustion processes, but we cannot be sure this will always be true in the future.

Distribution and Inequality

One of the most interesting and difficult questions in the evolutionary development of society is the change which takes place in the distributions—among individuals, families, or significant groups like classes or nations—of various aggregates which are significant in the system, like wealth or income, and how these changes are related to the institutions of society itself. The concepts of distribution and of inequality exist in biological systems, but it seems not to bother anybody there and does not receive a great deal of attention. Nevertheless, any ecosystem has a variety of niches—some for big things, some for small things, some for middle-sized things—so that there is a great variety of size ranging from the virus up to the elephant or the sequoia. We could certainly postulate a size distribution of members of different species for any given ecosystem. What determines this, as far as I know, has received very little attention from biologists. It clearly has something to do with the shapes of the big things; little things find niches in the cracks, that is, the spaces which are not occupied between the bigger things. The fact that a tree trunk, for instance, occupies far less area than its branches means that there are niches for bushes underneath the trees. The fact that things that are too densely spaced lose light or water, and other things (even for big things there is some optimum density of spacing) means that smaller things can occupy spaces between the bigger things, and still smaller things the spaces between the smaller things. There is something like this in social systems, where there is a tendency for large organizations to leave spaces between them in which smaller organizations flourish: The corner grocery still survives in the cracks of the supermarket, the hippies in old mining towns, pacifists in churches, radicals in universities, families in leisure time, and so on.

Distribution of Income Versus Wealth

Economists are particularly interested in the distribution of income (flows of valuable goods) and wealth (stocks of valuable goods). In a certain sense all income is derived from wealth, and wealth is measured by the discounted income derived from it, so the two are closely related. If indeed we included human capital under wealth—that is, property in individuals' minds and bodies from which wages are derived as income—the distribution of wealth and of income would be very similar. There still would be some differences as a result of different rates of return on different items of wealth.

The distribution of wealth is a result of two continuing social processes: the processes of inheritance and of lifetime accumulations. An individual whose income (or production) is persistently in excess of expenditure (or consumption) over his or her lifetime will accumulate wealth. Losses in value of wealth are counted as negative income. When an individual dies his wealth has to be distributed in some way among the living. The dynamics of the distribution of wealth depend very much on the laws and customs of inheritance. In most societies inheritance is to a very large extent confined to the family. If primogeniture is the rule (in which the eldest son inherits all the wealth of the father, or even of both parents), wealth will tend to remain unequal and concentrated in a few hands. If the practice is to distribute estates equally among all children, this will lead to more equal distribution of wealth, particularly if the wealthy have a lot of children. If the wealthy only have a few children, or if they marry each other, as is frequently the case, this tends to lead to a concentration of wealth and inequality, and this again is a very frequent condition.

The "Matthew Principle"

There is a principle, furthermore, sometimes called the "Matthew principle" (from the famous text "for whosoever hath, to him shall be given"),[3] implying that the rich find it easier to accumulate than do the poor. The larger one's income, the easier it is to get expenditure below it—that is, to save; whereas the smaller the income, the harder it becomes to save because the demands of sheer subsistence tend to gobble up all the income that is available. The very poor indeed nearly always dissave—that is, they spend more than their income, and either run down whatever capital they may have or run into debt, which is negative wealth. It is not surprising that equality is unstable and that there does seem to be something like an equilibrium degree of inequality which is hard, though not impossible, to change. Even the distribution of income in socialist countries, with the possible exception of China, is not markedly different from what it is in capitalist countries, particularly if geographical differences in income are taken into account.

Probably the most effective means of shifting the distribution of wealth and income toward greater equality is by developing a system of social inheritance which bypasses the family. This includes such things as public education, Head Start, welfare payments, negative income taxes, and so on, which in effect give those who otherwise would be poor an inheritance which depends only on their being a member of the society, not of a particular family. Even this, however, has fairly sharp limits simply because virtually no society is willing to give up the family as the major institution for the production and the training of children, and the family inheritance not only in the more ordinary forms of economic wealth, but in culture, language, habits, religion, ethics, and "know-whom"—that is, personal acquaintance—is still of overwhelming importance.

Taxation and Distribution

The government tax and expenditure system always has some kind of impact on the distribution both of wealth and of income. It may move it either toward or away from whatever ideal of justice and distribution we postulate. Progressive taxation, which means in general that the proportion of income paid in taxes rises with larger incomes, is an important redistributive device which has developed within the last 100 years or so, mainly in Western societies. The income tax is a peculiarly useful instrument for progressive taxation, although any tax system can be progressive if it falls more heavily on those goods which are particularly purchased by the rich and avoids taxing those which are purchased by the poor. A system of commodity taxation, for instance, which avoids taxing basic foodstuffs and simple clothing and concentrates on luxury goods which are purchased only by the rich, will have a progressive impact. It is very easy, however, for the tax system to be regressive, where the poor pay a larger share of their income than the rich. Preindustrial tax systems are usually of this kind. Indeed, it was only with the coming of science-based technology that progressive taxation seems to have become politically feasible.

If progressivity is overdone, of course, it may have adverse effects on productivity and development. On the whole it is the rich who know how to change and develop; the poor are too busy keeping body and soul together, and they have very little freedom of action. Soaking the rich too much, therefore, may in the long run injure the poor, as it may lead into a stagnant society. The certainty of taxation in this respect may have much more impact than its amount, for uncertainty is a great deterrent to investment and innovation.

Expenditures also may have distributive effects. If the public purse is used to build palaces and castles and to fight wars, on the whole this will have regressive effects and will concentrate wealth and income toward the rich and the rulers. If it is used to subsidize education, to provide "negative taxes" for the poor in the form of welfare payments or food stamps, if it subsidizes the production of those things which the poor buy, then it may have a progressive effect.

In the United States the overall tax expenditure system seems to be remarkably neutral over a large range of incomes. Studies at the Brookings Institution[4] suggest that perhaps in the middle 80 or 90 percent range of incomes families pay about the same portion of their income in combined federal, state, and local taxes. The progressive elements of the federal tax are offset by the regressive elements of state and local taxes. For the bottom 10 percent, however, there is not much doubt that the system is highly progressive and that the poor are substantially subsidized. For the top 5 percent, it also seems to be progressive, as the top 5 percent does pay a larger proportion of its income into taxes than the middle.

Development and Distribution

Developmental processes are almost certain to increase inequality, particularly in their early stages. Development results mainly from mutations in the rate of increase of knowledge and know-how structure of the human race. This takes place in particular times and places, and takes place in the minds of particular individuals, such as inventors, innovators, entrepreneurs, and scientists. The great evolutionary development of the last 200 years has undoubtedly increased world inequality. Figures are not available, but one suspects that 200 years ago in terms of per capita real income or wealth, the richest countries were not more than five times as rich as the poorest countries, though Adam Smith does say that in Europe "the accommodation (of an industrious and frugal peasant) exceeds that of many an African king."[5] Today the richest countries in terms of per capita real income are perhaps forty times as rich as the poorest countries.

The reason for this increasing inequality is not "exploitation" in any crude sense, in the sense that is that the poor have been producing a lot and the rich have been taking it away from them. This does not rule out the possibility of more subtle forms of exploitation in terms of the rich cultures preventing the poor cultures from adapting to increasing productivity. But the main reason for the increasing inequality is simply that the rich countries have been getting richer faster and longer than the poor countries, because the mutations which have led to increasing productivity took place first in the countries which are now rich and are taking a long time to spread to the poor countries for a great variety of reasons, some of which are connected with the internal culture of these countries and some with the external impacts of the rich countries on them.

Labor, Land, and Capital as Factors of Distribution

I argued earlier that the traditional "factors of production"—labor, land, and capital—are not useful aggregates when it comes to understanding the processes of production. They are significant categories, however, when it comes to understanding distribution, though even from this point of view they are also very heterogeneous. Human activity together with the price structure produces a set of real earnings per hour, real rents per acre, and real profit or interest percent per annum. Earnings per hour is the increase in command over real goods and services which results from a person-hour of human activity. This may include direct domestic production of things for personal use, as when we cook a dinner which we then eat. This involves, incidentally, applying the know-how of the cook, the energy of the stove, and raw food materials for the production of a plate of dinner. Earnings also take the form of wages, usually money paid by an employer for activity measured either in time (hours) or in product, as in piecework, at the employer's discretion. The money wage is then spent by the worker on commodities.

An important aspect of society is the division of the total product into earnings income (sometimes called labor income), which accrues to people as a result of time spent in economic activity directly, and nonearnings income which includes income from the ownership of nonpersonal capital like buildings, stocks of goods, and so on, as profit and interest. This division depends in considerable degree on the relative price structure, and this in turn depends on rates of time discount as reflected in profit and interest rates in a society. These are phenomena which are found, if at all, only in a most primitive form in biological ecosystems, and they add greatly to the complexity of societal ecosystems. Whether the economic system produces equilibrium values for wages or earnings incomes, rents, and profit and interest rates is a critical question which is by no means fully resolved.

Space and Time as Factors

In thinking about economic production, we have to go beyond our three factors of know-how, energy, and materials, to add the factors of space and time. All productive processes involve space, which is likely to be scarce and a limiting factor in many cases, and therefore will command a price because it has some kind of alternative cost, though a rather peculiar one. The time factor is even trickier and has received a great deal of attention from economists. All productive processes take time, in the sense that we cannot have today what we can have tomorrow. All capital accumulation involves postponement of some kind of consumption, because accumulation consists of products not yet consumed or depreciated. The rate of profit or interest, expressed as a percent per annum, describes the rate of exchange between present and future goods at different dates. If the rate of interest is 5 percent per annum in real terms, $100 worth of goods today is exchanged for $105 worth of goods at this time next year, and $110.25 worth of goods two years from now, and so on. Asking "Why is there a rate of interest?" is the same as asking "Why is it not zero?" and the answer seems to be, in the terms of the great American economist Irving Fisher, that either there is impatience—we would rather have $100 now than $105 next year—or there may be a productivity of "waiting" in that processes of production themselves involve time and cannot be hurried. The maturing of wines is a classic example, for the value of the wine increases with age. As in all processes, we would have less product, or a less valued product, if we tried to have it earlier. In any process indeed there is likely to be an optimum period of production in the sense that we will have less if we try to have it either too early or too late. The best wine eventually turns into vinegar, and delay may diminish the product itself. These phenomena do not seem to have very clear counterparts in biological ecosystems because of the absence there of revisable images of the future on anything but the very narrowest time scale, and the absence of anything beyond the most primitive forms of decision.

The Evolution of Finance and Interest

The evolution of financial instruments, such as interest-bearing loans and bonds, shares of stock, bank deposits, credit cards, and so on, is a very interesting and complex stream of human history. The pattern, however, follows the ordinary evolutionary course. Soon after exchange and specialized production begin, especially of specialized merchants, a niche arises in the system for financial institutions of some kind because we cannot have trade without property in the things traded. These properties, whether by inheritance or other means, often fall into the hands of people who do not want or do not have the skills for trading;

then there are clear payoffs for everybody for some sort of devices for separating the actual ownership or equity in traded goods from their control. It is not surprising that we get loans and financial contracts of increasing complexity, though it still has to be explained how these generate interest and profit. Then the principle continues that as each niche is filled for a new species of financial implement, this tends to create niches for more complex ones. As early as ancient Greek civilization we get money in many forms, the beginning of paper credit, bills of exchange, promises to pay various things, and the like. The Chinese had paper money quite early. Quite elaborate banking and financial institutions developed in the European Middle Ages. From the seventeenth century on we have a continual creation of new financial species—bank notes; futures contracts (which are promises to pay commodities rather than money); promises to pay other financial instruments; corporations with shares of stock in increasing variety such as preferred shares, ordinary shares, and so on; until we reach the great variety of species of financial instruments and transactions that we find today.

Historically, however, the financial system has been troubled for a long time with the problem of legitimacy. In the minds of many people, especially those who are not familiar with the financial system, the taking of interest on loans and other financial instruments has been suspect on moral grounds. This goes back at least to Aristotle, or even further back to the "years of jubilee" among the ancient Israelites when all debts were supposed to be forgiven, up to the prohibitions of usury and the various excuses made to get around it in the Middle Ages in Christian Europe and even more rigorously in Islam. In fact to many people interest seems like getting something for nothing, and its role in society has frequently been misunderstood by philosophers, theologians, and even politicians. This environment of illegitimacy reaches its climax, perhaps, in Marx and the communist countries, where capital markets, except in a very few restricted cases, have lost all legitimacy and their functions have been taken over by the state. This is a good example of how the size of a niche depends on its total environment, political and social as well as economic and even biological and physical. If the old stock exchange in Leningrad is now a Palace of Culture and Rest, this in no way contradicts the general evolutionary pattern. The niche for it closed because of changes in the structure of political power and of moral legitimacy.

Notes

1. Adam Smith, *The Wealth of Nations*, Book I, Chapter VI.

2. Richard G. Wilkinson, *Poverty and Progress: An Ecological Perspective on Economic Development* (New York: Praeger, 1973).

3. Matthew 13:12.

4. Joseph A. Pechman and Benjamin A. Okner, *Who Bears the Tax Burden?* (Washington, D.C.: Brookings Institution, 1974).

5. Adam Smith, *The Wealth of Nations* (New York: Random House/Modern Library Edition), Book I, Ch. 1, p. 12.

CHAPTER 3

Evolutionary and "Mainline" Economics

We have seen in the two previous chapters how evolutionary models can be applied to economic life and economic theory. We should now go on to ask the question as to how far this represents a change in the development of economic thought, and how far it is integrated with the existing history of economics. Is evolutionary economics a development in the ongoing stream of economics, or does it represent some revolutionary change in direction?

Economics as an Old Science

Economics has some claims to be the second, or perhaps the third oldest of the sciences, after astronomy and physics. Adam Smith, the Newton of economics, was a contemporary of Linnaeus, the great taxonomist. In his *Wealth of Nations*, 1776, he transformed it from a collection of sporadic insights about particular phenomena into an organized body of theory, not all of it equally valid, but capable of continual refine ment and modification over the succeeding 200 years. Economics, though younger than physics (at least Newtonian physics), is considerably older than chemistry, which only reached its basic theoretical formulation with Dalton, who was a contemporary of Ricardo. It is much older than theoretical biology, which really dates from Darwin, a hundred years after Adam Smith. We cannot expect the classical economists, such as Smith,[1] Malthus,[2] Ricardo,[3] J. S. Mill,[4] and even Karl Marx,[5] all of whose work preceded Darwin,[6] to be explicitly aware of the importance of natural selection and mutation, and we would certainly not expect them to have any explicit evolutionary models. Nevertheless, it is no accident that it was reading Malthus "for pleasure" one evening that gave Darwin the idea of natural selection, for an implicit evolutionary model is very strong in classical economics, especially in Adam Smith and Malthus. It is a little less strong perhaps in Ricardo, and quite weak in Marx, who derives his dynamics from a Hegelian model of dialectical interaction, which, as we have seen, is only a small part of the evolutionary process.

Marshall as an Evolutionist

The implicit evolutionary model returns with full force in Alfred Marshall's *Principles of Economics.*[7] He was familiar with Darwin, but he was never able to incorporate the evolutionary insights explicitly into his formal theory, even though he had a strong ambition to do so. He felt strongly that it was biology, rather than Newtonian mechanics, which should be the model of economics. Yet in his day biological theory had not really advanced to the point where it could be integrated into economic models. The implicit evolutionary model in Marshall, however, is very strong. His equilibrium mechanical models of supply and demand he always regards as mere stepping stones toward a richer dynamic evolutionary theory.

Mechanical Models: Walras and Samuelson

In Walras,[8] unfortunately, the clarification of the explicit equilibrium model of price theory, an important achievement in itself, had the effect of diminishing the force of the implicit evolutionary model to the point where it almost disappears. Unfortunately, the twentieth-century mainline of economics followed Walras a good deal more than it did Marshall, with concentration on the equilibrium concept almost to the exclusion of evolutionary change.

With the development of econometrics and what might be called Samuelsonian dynamics,[9] with models essentially involving stable parameters and a dynamic based on stable difference or differential equations, mainline economics became even more Newtonian and less Darwinian. It became almost obsessed with mechanical models analogous to those of celestial mechanics and was remarkably insensitive to the possibility of unexpected and unpredictable parametric change. A striking example of this is an article by Samuelson in *The New*

Republic[10] in 1944, predicting 12 million unemployed six months after the end of the war. This prediction, fortunately, was completely false because it was based on the parameters of the 1930s, and there was a marked change in parameters of the system between the 1930s and the 1940s. The basic parameters of the system, however, were again rather stable between about 1950 and 1973, so that the econometric projections were fairly successful until OPEC and the oil embargo churned things up again.

Evolution and Development: Schumpeter

In the same period, however, the Newtonian mechanical models were not at all successful in handling the problem of economic development, which is, after all, a highly evolutionary process. Evolution and development indeed are almost the same word. Joseph Schumpeter,[11] with his theory of economic development, a pioneer in development theory, has strong claims to be identified as an evolutionary economist. He was particularly well aware of the great importance of mutation in terms of invention, innovation, and entrepreneurship, especially the latter. He had a strong sense also of how innovation introduced new niches into the system and also led to the collapse of some old ones. Indeed, he saw clearly that the new niches for new commodities and new methods could not be created unless some of the old ones were allowed to collapse, and that the protection of old niches, which was a not inconsiderable part of government policy, could very well prevent the development and the filling of the new ones. In his *Capitalism, Socialism, and Democracy*,[12] he has a strong sense of the whole social-ecological framework within which economic institutions rise and fall, and his view that the institutions of capitalism could not generate that social framework in terms of legitimacy which alone could lead to their survival, while it may not be entirely true, was a profound insight and highly consistent with an ecological-evolutionary view of social dynamics.

Unfortunately, Schumpeter's insights seem to have been admired and then laid to one side. Development theory in the last thirty years has concentrated very heavily on mechanical models involving constant parameters, such as capital-income ratios or equilibrium rates of growth of some kind, following R. F. Harrod[13] and Evsey Domar.[14] It has, therefore, not been able to explain the enormous differences in different societies, mainly the result of noneconomic factors in the general social ecosystem, nor has it been able to deal with the political instabilities and policies which have often had such disastrous effects on the developmental process.

Evolutionary Economics Makes More Explicit an Old, Implicit Tradition in Economic Thought

I would argue, therefore, that evolutionary economics is not something foreign to the general development of economic thought, that in an implicit form at any rate it has been there almost from the beginning, certainly from Adam Smith, and that while it has from time to time been diverted by the more explicit attractiveness of mechanical and dialectical models, it has continued as an ongoing tradition in economic thought. I regard evolutionary economics, therefore, as simply making more explicit what has been implicit in economic thought for a very long time. Evolutionary economics is itself evolutionary rather than revolutionary. It is a mutation which would strengthen the whole ecosystem of economic thought and make it richer and more varied. It does not exclude the more mechanical systems which have their value—indeed, a great value—in those periods when parameters are fairly stable, and which indeed are a necessary prelude to the understanding of the larger and more complex evolutionary systems, but it goes beyond them into a larger temporal framework.

Evolutionary Mathematics as Topological Rather Than Numerical

It must be admitted that the evolutionary model has its weaknesses. It is not easy to make it completely explicit, and indeed this is still a task for the future. It resists simple mathematization, partly one suspects because the mathematics for it has not been written. Newtonian and Cartesian numerical mathematics, which has dominated economics, is unsuitable to the more structural and topological relations of evolutionary systems, except insofar as the topological relations can be mapped into numerical relations. But the cardinal numbers are a property of the human imagination rather than of the real world, which consists of the topology of shapes and relative sizes rather than of numbers. Topological models which relate structural forms may be far closer to the real world than quantitative equations which are united only by an equality of number. Evolution involves a richness of interaction which cannot be expressed by Cartesian-Newtonian mathematics, with its appalling paucity of verbs and its insistence that minus-minus is plus. Not doing harm is not the same as doing good! This does mean, however, that the numerologists, who are obsessed with quantification often far beyond the point where it is meaningful, will find evolutionary theory vague and "literary," for this may just reflect the present state of its mathematical development.

Evolutionary and Standard Price Theory: Supply and Demand

We have seen in the previous chapter that price theory can be fitted into an evolutionary framework with great ease, for there is implicit in it an ecological interaction of commodities which continually exercises a strong selective process. Those commodities are selected which satisfy an effective demand sufficient to make their production normally advantageous, and those commodities move toward extinction which fail to satisfy this criterion. Into this system mutation constantly intrudes in the form of invention, new processes, new technologies, new commodities, new tastes, and new demands. Equilibrium in such a system is a useful intellectual construct, even though it is never found in the real world. It defines a moving target which constantly changes as it is pursued. Marshall's long-run equilibrium, as we have seen, is a concept virtually identical with that of a climactic ecosystem, in which the implications of all the existing ecological parameters are worked out. The long-run equilibrium, however, like the climactic ecosystem, is continually subject itself to shifts as a result of mutations in the underlying parameters of the system, whether technological or psychological.

It remains to show how the mathematical and graphical apparatus of price theory, particularly of supply and demand, can be derived from the ecological-evolutionary model. Let us take a single commodity, say wheat. In Figure 1 we show the relation of the production of wheat to its total stock on the curve SS′ and the relation of the consumption of wheat to its total stock on the curve DD′. We measure the total stock in the reverse of the usual convention, for reasons which will be apparent in a moment, with a high stock at the bottom of the figure and a low stock at the top. We measure stock vertically along the line OA, but it is high at the bottom and falls as we move toward A. We measure production and consumption along the line OB; each of them rises as we move toward B. This is a basic ecological model, where production is equivalent to births—that is, additions to the total stock; consumption is equivalent to deaths—that is, subtractions from the total stock. The production and consumption curves intersect at E, which is the equilibrium point at which production and consumption are equal, and therefore the total stock is neither rising nor falling. Suppose that point A represents a zero stock and that at the equilibrium stock AF (which just occupies its "niche") production and consumption are both equal to FE. When the total stock is below the equilibrium level, say at AF_1, consumption is F_1D_1, production is F_1S_1, there is an excess of production over consumption equal to D_1S_1 and the total stock is increasing—that is, moving from F_1 toward F. If the total stock is at AF_2, greater than the equilibrium level, production will be F_2S_2, consumption will be F_2D_2, there will be an excess consumption over production equal to S_2D_2 and the stock will fall, again toward F. The equilibrium, therefore, under these circumstances is stable.

In biological systems, the relation between the total stock (population) and production (births) or consumption (deaths) is mediated through food shortages, housing shortages, predation, maternal care, and a large number of other variables. In the economic system it is mediated almost entirely through the effect on price, though we should not rule out other effects, such as storage and spoilage costs, anticipations of price, and so on. The relationship is shown in Figure 2. If the stock of wheat were zero, the price would be extremely high. As the stock of wheat rises, the price falls in the market, simply because the larger the stock of wheat which has to be held in the market, the more people have to be "bribed" by a low price to hold this stock, preferences being unchanged. At some point H the stock of wheat is so high that the price is zero. With still larger stocks the price would become negative—that is, people would have to be paid to increase their stock of wheat—but this position is never reached in practice. Then in Figure 1 we can now draw a line PP' parallel to OA on which we can write the price of wheat that corresponds to each stock in Figure 2. If the price-stock relationship in Figure 2 were a straight line, then the price of wheat would increase in regular intervals as we went from P to P'. If we substitute PP' for the line OA, Figure 1 now becomes a conventional long-run demand and supply

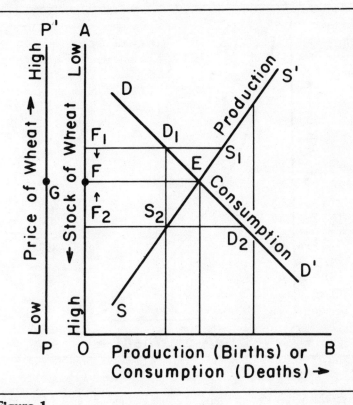

Figure 1

curve, with SS' the supply, DD' the demand, and an equilibrium price equal to PG.

Marshall's Dynamics

Marshall had an approach to the problem of adjustments toward equilibrium of the price system somewhat different from the one presented in Figure 1, which is essentially that of Walras. This is shown in Figure 3. As before we measure production or consumption along OB, price now along OA. SS' and DD' are the long-run supply and demand curves intersecting at the equilibrium point at E. It is then argued that if

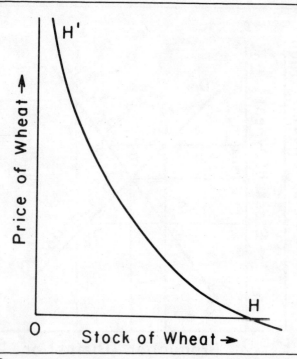

Figure 2

actual production were less than the equilibrium level $OB_e(= FE)$—say, at OB_1—the actual price would be B_1D_1, assuming that all that was produced would have to be sold. Suppliers, however, would be willing to supply this amount at a price B_1S_1, this being the supply price—that is, the price at which people would be willing to supply OB_1. In this case there would be an excess of the demand price, which would be the actual price, over the supply price. This would mean that the suppliers would be unusually well rewarded and would receive economic rents. In a competitive occupation in which there were no obstacles, either to entry or to exit from the occupation, these excess rewards would attract resources into the occupation and production would rise; as it rose the demand price at which it could be sold would fall, the supply price would rise until the demand price and the supply price were equal at E, both being B_eE, and production would no longer expand. Similarly, if production were greater than at the equilibrium level—say, at OB_2—the actual price or demand price would be B_2D_2, the supply price would be greater than this at B_2S_2, the producers would be underpaid, they would leave the occupation, and production would shrink; as it shrank the demand or actual price would rise, the supply price would fall, until they were equal again at E, at which point the shrinkage in production would cease. Ironically enough, in spite of the fact that Marshall had much more of an evolutionary point of view than Walras, his actual model of equilibrium—derived essentially from Adam Smith—is much less adaptable to the ecological-evolutionary mode, which operates mainly through the impact of the rise and fall of stocks or population on the birth (production) or death (consumption) rates. The Marshallian dynamics would emphasize the prosperity or adversity of the populations as a factor affecting their growth or decline. Small populations are prosperous and therefore grow; large populations are miserable and therefore decline. In the case of commodities, if one industry is "too small" it will be unusually prosperous, resources will come into it from other industries; and if it is "too large" it will be relatively unprosperous and resources will flow out of it. There is a certain parallel to this in biological systems, in that a species which has a population well below its equilibrium level as it expands will pass more of the ultimate resources of the system in terms of materials and energy through its population, which may of course mean fewer resources for other species.

Equilibrium as a Minimization of Stress

A more fundamental consideration is that of the nature of the response of systems to some kind of stress. Equilibrium theory supposes that there is some position of the system at which stress is so low that the system does not change. If the system is not at equilibrium, it means that stress on it is making for change. If the equilibrium is a stable one, these changes would move the system toward equilibrium. We could almost do without the equilibrium concept if we suppose that we can identify in the first place the strains on the system making for change, in the second place the relation between these strains and the changes which will ensue, and in the third place the impact of the changes on the strain itself. We could perfectly well visualize a system that had no equilibrium, but in

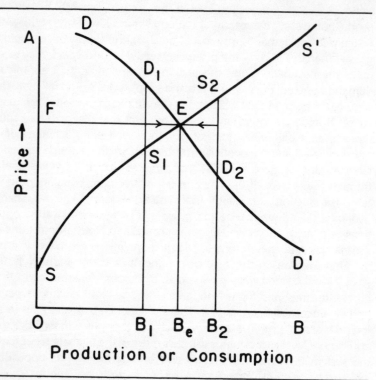

Figure 3

which the change took place continually, faster if the reaction to strain
and the changes which are produced by it actually increase the strain,
and slower where the system's reaction to strain diminishes the strain. In
fact, this is what the world is like. It never has exhibited an equilibrium,
although there are enough quasiequilibria to justify the use of the concept.

The "Weakest Link" Model of Adjustment to Stress

The critical question here is: What adjusts when there is a strain on
the system? The obvious answer to this is, of course, that what adjusts is
the adjustable and if some things are not adjustable, then other things
will have to adjust. It might be called the "weakest link" model; when

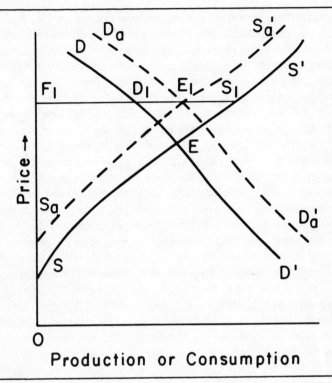

Figure 4

there is strain on the system it "gives" at the weakest or most adjustable point. What is the weakest point of the system, however, is often quite hard to determine, particularly in advance. In the case of price theory this problem is illustrated in Figure 4. Here we go back to the model of Figure 1. Let us suppose that the price is OF_1, which is above the equilibrium price, so that there is an excess supply D_1S_1; with a consequent increase in stocks the suppliers are unable to dispose of all of their product. In conventional price theory we assume that this will produce a fall in the price, as suppliers who are accumulating unwanted stocks will unload by offering bargains to buyers, and that this will go on until we get to E, at which the excess supply disappears.

Suppose now, however, that prices are not adjustable, that, for instance, we have price control which makes illegal any offer to sell at a lower price than OF_1. There may of course be black markets—under these circumstances there usually are—and the overall price may edge downward. But other reactions may also take place. With an excess supply there is a strong incentive on the part of the suppliers to increase demand, and they can do this by advertising and undertaking selling costs. If the demanders are easily persuaded, the demand curve may easily move from DD' to D_aD_a', thus reducing the excess supply. There also, however, may be changes in supply. Where there are excess supplies there are no incentives to improve production or to lower costs, costs indeed may rise, at least relative to other commodities; there will be very little activity devoted to cost reduction. The supply curve, therefore, may move to the dotted line S_aS_a', and we have a new equilibrium at E_1 at the rigid price OF_1. This situation is by no means unrealistic under conditions of government regulation of prices in which these other adjustments may be easier than price adjustments. The system, again, gives at its weakest point. In this case the adjustments in supply and demand will reduce the stress and get rid of the excess supply. Similarly, if the price is fixed below the equilibrium level, there would be an excess demand this will encourage cost reduction and technical change (for there is no selling problem) and supply will fall, with the supply curve moving to the right. The excess demand will also discourage selling cost, which may lower the demand, and we may end up again with an equilibrium at the rigid price.

System Breaks and Continuous Strain

A fundamental principle here is that strain may increase up to a point without any changes; then there is a very sudden change at the breaking point. This is sometimes called a "system break." Price control is a good example of this. If the controlled legal prices are not very different from the equilibrium set, there will be some excess demands and supplies, but these will be tolerated and taken care of by other adjustments, such a queuing, rationing, and so on. If, however, the structure of legal prices gets too far out of line with the equilibrium levels, the prices themselves will adjust either through the development of black markets or by pressures on government to abolish or to modify the price control system itself. The evolutionary process here is one in which a strain increases in a system until at some point something gives, and there is a change; this change, however, will redistribute the strain on other parts of the system, and increase the strain on other weak points to the point where they give, and so on continuously. Every time we solve one problem we create three others and change, therefore, is usually self-perpetuating.

Cyclical Systems: The Cobweb Theorem and Dialectical Cycles

Sometimes indeed we seem to get cyclical changes around some equilibrium value, which may or may not converge. A famous example of this is the so-called cobweb theorem in economics, illustrated in Figures 5 and 6. Here we suppose a commodity—say, with an annual harvest. The supply curve then relates the production of one year to the price of the previous year, and the demand curve relates the price of each year to the output of that year. The demand curve then shows what price will correspond to each current annual output, the supply curve shows the next year's production in response to the previous year's price. Suppose we start off at D_1, a harvest of F_1D_1, and a price of OF_1. The price OF_1 produces a harvest F_1S_2 the next year at a price of OF_2, which produces a harvest of F_2S_3 the next year at a price of OF_3; we could go on in an exploding cycle. Exploding cycles cannot, of course, last for very long. They reach some kind of boundary or breaking point and may even destroy the system. Figure 6 shows a similar cycle which converges to the equilibrium point at E. If the demand and supply curves are symmetrical, the cycle will be persistent and will go on indefinitely. Cycles of this kind have not been unknown, for instance, in hog production, though they have become increasingly rarer with government intervention and the widening of the market. Rather similar cycles are found in natural ecosystems that are very sparse, such as the cycle in the population of the Arctic hare; they are rare in complex systems. Political cycles of liberalism and conservatism and moral cycles of puritanism and licentiousness are also not uncommon in the history of societies. They could almost be called dialectical cycles, in which the position of the system creates a sufficient strain so that there is a large change to a somewhat opposite position, which however also creates strain until we get another

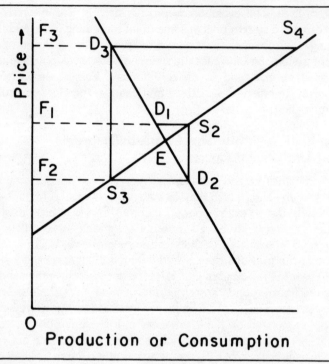

Figure 5

large change back to where we were before. The history of revolutions exhibits some interesting parallels to this kind of model. Thus, the French Revolution produced Napoleon and the Russian Revolution, Stalin.

Microeconomics and the Theory of Maximizing Behavior

It is clear that the evolutionary perspective fits comfortably into the mainstream of price theory in economics. The next question is: What would be its impact on microeconomics at the level of the theory of the firm and the household? This is an important part of the standard economics textbook. Historically, this theory does not go much before W. S. Jevons and Alfred Marshall and the development of the marginal

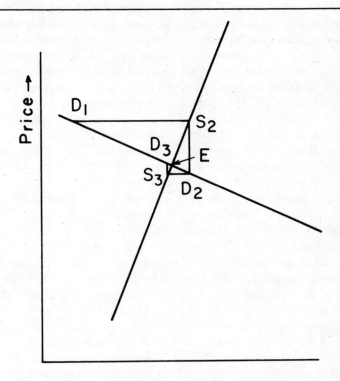

Production or Consumption

Figure 6

analysis. Its basic assumption is that there is an equilibrium position of any particular economic organization, whether a firm or a household, based on the assumption of the maximization of some measure or indicator of economic welfare. In the case of the household this is supposed to be a subjective feeling of utility or satisfaction. In the first approximation theory of the firm this is assumed to be some measure of profits.

This leads directly into the theory of maximizing behavior. Behavior is a change in the state of the organism or organization. The theory states that behavior is governed by choice or decision. This involves selecting the "best" over a range of alternative images of the future, each of which is perceived to be practicable, the best being defined as that at which the "maximand" or the "objective"—whatever it is that is maximized—is the greatest over the whole range of alternatives. This discrete pattern of an agenda of choice is then often assumed to be continuous over what might be called an agenda field, in as many dimensions as there are variables in the description of the state of the system. In economic theory these variables are assumed to be such things as quantities of commodities bought, sold, produced, consumed, or held in a stock, and the prices at which offers are made to buy and sell. The decision maker is supposed to be able to identify each point on the field in terms of at least an ordinal number, which is an indicator of some maximand such as utility or profits. Any move which increases this maximand will be made until we reach a maximum, at which point a move in any direction will lower the maximand. We think of the process as climbing up the "maximand hill." We will make any move that takes us "up." As we keep on going up, however, we eventually get to the top—that is, the maximum position which is supposed to be the equilibrium, much as the top of the mountain is the equilibrium position of a mountain climber. The analogy is a dangerous one, for the mountain climber has to come down again, whereas economic man or woman apparently stays at the top of the utility mountain and lives happily ever afterward.

The analysis is further refined by supposing that we can divide the field of conceivable positions of the organization into two parts: those which are feasible and those which are not, divided by what is called a "possibility boundary," within which the organization has a choice, beyond which it does not. We can think of the possibility boundary as a fence going over the side of the maximand hill. The highest position on the fence is now the significant maximum. The fact that there may be preferred positions beyond the fence is irrelevant. This illustrates an interesting difference between the economist's view of human behavior and the psychologist's. What the economist calls equilibrium—that is, the highest point on the possibility fence—a psychologist calls frustration, as we are supposed to kick and scream when we reach the fence because we cannot get over it.

The Marginal Analysis

The theory of maximization, or of maximizing behavior, produced the marginal analysis. This is a set of elegant mathematical conclusions from the principle that everybody does what he thinks is best at the time. Thus, if we can divide a description of the state of the organization into things that have negative utility (costs) and into things which have positive utility (revenues or benefits), it is easy to derive the proposition that at the maximum point marginal costs are equal to marginal revenues or benefits. This leads into some quite interesting conclusions about the reactions of an economic organization to changes in its price environment. It can be shown not only that there is a high probability that a rise in price will discourage purchase and consumption and will encourage sales and production, but we can even specify that characteristics of the underlying utility functions give us varying degrees of responsiveness, and even the circumstances under which responsiveness might be perverse and a rise in price would increase purchases or diminish sales, as, for instance, sometimes happens in speculative markets or in the case of commodities which have symbolic value, such as diamonds.[15]

The Evolutionary Model of Behavior as Growth and Production

All this elegance is not to be despised, and I would certainly argue that the theory of maximizing behavior has been a powerful instrument in clarifying our images of what might be called formal rationality, and that this is at least a common enough norm so that the conclusions of the theory throw some light on the real world. The evolutionary perspective, however, does demand an image of the dynamics of individual organisms and organizations which goes far beyond the special case or "ideal type," as Max Weber might call it, of the theory of maximizing behavior. The theory of maximizing behavior and the marginal analysis is essentially "Newtonian." It is a mechanical, not an evolutionary, model. The evolutionary model sees the organism or organization not as an equilibrium system, although there are important quasi-equilibrium conditions, as in homeostasis in the biological organism and corresponding conditions in a social or economic organization. Basically, however, as we have seen, the evolutionary perspective sees the individual organism as originating from a cluster of genetic information and instructions; for instance, in the fertilized egg in the case of a living organism or in the basic idea, contract, constitution, or charter in the case of the social organization. From this original genetic "know-how" base the organism or organization proceeds to grow by the processes we have observed, capturing energy to transport and transform materials, to code further information and instructions in an ongoing developmental process. In such development the state of the organism or organization never exhibits a true equilibrium but is always subject to constant change, guided by the instructions and pattern of the genetic material. In the case of biological organisms this constant change develops first the fetus, then the baby, the child, the adult, and finally leads into aging and death.

Social Organizations in Constant Disequilibrium

Social organizations are more complex. They are capable of re-creating genetic material along the way in a manner that seems to be impossible with biological organizations, except perhaps by human intervention, as with recombinant DNA. They experience renewals and genetic transformations as people come into them with new ideas and as they respond in the knowledge and know-how structure to changing circumstances. We see this, for instance, in how a nation changes in character in the course of its history while maintaining continuity, moving from loose feudal obligations into absolute monarchy, into oligarchy, into constitutional democracy, into and out of tyranny, into and one hopes out of centrally planned economies, and so on. The family begins with some kind of contract between a man and a woman, which may be informal and highly unspecified, or which may be formalized in a marriage; if they have children, the number in the family increases, everybody in the family ages year by year and becomes in effect a different being. The family changes continuously; it has no equilibrium whatever. A particular family eventually disintegrates as the children leave home, as the parents die, the children marry and form new families, and so on.

Homeostasis

In this incessant "Heraclitian flux," what remains of any kind of equilibrium theory? The answer seems to be that it may be useful to describe states of the organism which are stable enough over time so that change, at least for short periods, can be neglected. We see this, for instance, in the theory of homeostasis in the biological organism, over short periods in which aging can be neglected. Living organisms have something approaching an equilibrium state and have a good deal of apparatus for maintaining it. In order to operate they require stocks of stored energy; for instance, in ATP. As this is diminished by their activity it has to be replaced from food, so activity designed to produce a reasonable equilibrium state here obviously has great survival value. This is why organisms get hungry and thirsty, why food search is genetically built into a great deal of animal behavior, why excretion is necessary, and why temperatures have to be sustained. In the so-called warm-blooded animals, for instance, there is an elaborate apparatus of thermostats to keep the blood temperature within a very narrow range, which is presumably the most efficient range for bodily processes. An organism that gets either too hot or too cold will take all sorts of steps to correct this situation through its cybernetic apparatuses.[16]

Behavior as Maintenance of State

The theory of homeostasis can also be applied to social and economic organizations. In each case it is not unreasonable to define a "state" of the organization as represented by a position statement or some kind of extended balance sheet and to interpret the behavior of the organization in terms of maintaining this state. The state in economic terms is the capital stock, including in this not only material capital but human capital, states of mind, and so on. These states continually are eroded by consumption and depreciation and have to be maintained, therefore, by continual production and exchange, just as a biological organism has to maintain its state of energy by a continual throughput of food, water, and air. Thus, when I look into my sock drawer and discover that the ravages of time have diminished the number of viable socks, I go out and buy some more. As I do this my liquid assets shrink a little. If they shrink sufficiently, I have to replenish them by getting a job and earning money or perhaps by selling some little-wanted asset.

One could easily extend the homeostasis principle to states of mind: If I go to the opera, I create a state of mind which might be called "just having gone to the opera." In most cases this would be sufficiently strong so that I would be unlikely to go to an opera the next day. It depreciates, however, and, if I am a real opera fan, I may have to restore it by going to another opera in a few days. If I am not an opera fan, the state of just having been to an opera may last for months or even years. We can turn it around, of course, and define the state negatively as wanting to go to an opera and regard this as increasing; this would not make much difference. In the business firm, likewise, it is at least an interesting first approximation of its behavior to suppose that it maintains some homeostasis of the balance sheet. When it sells something, liquid assets increase and inventories diminish. In order to restore the previous state, the increase in liquid assets has to be spent for labor and raw materials and so on, which are organized in processes of production to restore the inventory. In all cases, of course, homeostasis depends on the existence of a perceptive apparatus, which perceives disproportions in the state of the organization and which has some kind of behavior patterns which can correct these disproportions.

Moving to Preferred States as "Maximization"

The theory of homeostasis is a very first approximation, for, as we have seen, organizations are subject to constant change, and the state which is maintained by a homeostatic apparatus itself continually changes. Here now we get closer to the maximizing behavior model, for if we ask what would induce an organism to move from one homeostatically maintained state to another, the answer presumably is that the one it moves to is "preferred." In the case of animals, this phenomenon is well known. Animals, for instance, migrate to more favorable environments, clearly under the impact of something like a utility function. We see this even in the most primitive forms of life. It is certainly not absurd to suppose that an amoeba has some kind of indifference curves, that it prefers a particle of food to a grain of sand, ingesting the one and rejecting the other, or even that it is sensitive to the effects of its movement, so that it will reverse its motion when the move is perceived as moving into a less favorable environment and continue to move forward when the move is perceived as into a more favorable environment.

Households and business firms likewise move from one homeostatic state to another that is preferred. These movements are of great importance in explaining, for instance, speculative behavior. The firm which operates in the wheat market, whose assets consist mainly of money or liquid assets of some form and wheat, or some kind of wheat delivery contracts, will constantly change its perception of its "ideal" balance sheet in the light of its expectations about the future of prices. If it expects the price of wheat to rise, it will tend to shift its assets into wheat by buying it and so drawing down its liquid assets. If it expects the price of wheat to fall, it will sell wheat and increase its liquid assets. This is why prices in speculative markets are so unstable and exhibit strong irregular fluctuations as expectations of the future change.

Do We Maximize the Hope of Gain or Minimize the Fear of Loss?

It is interesting now to inquire, in what sense do households maximize utility or firms maximize profits in conditions of constant change? The answer depends very much on the nature of the information system. If a wheat speculator changes his expectations of prices, this could be regarded as a change in the "know-how," or genetic structure of the organization; this is passed on as instructions to the various parts of the organization to behave in such a way that the asset structure changes in accordance with the change in the image of the future. In one sense maximization is a truism—that all decisions are believed to be for the best. Whether they in fact turn out to be for the best, however, is another matter altogether, for this depends on the accuracy—or in evolutionary terms, the survival value—of the changes—that is, mutations—in the know-how or genetic structure of the organization in response to information received from the environment. When everybody is supposed to maximize profits, how is it that so many organizations suffer losses or even become bankrupt? The answer is, of course, that their noogenetic structure—that is, their image of themselves, the environment and the world around them, and the future—may mutate in ways that do not lead to survival. This happens all the time in biological evolution: if a biogenetic mutation leads to survival it is simply good luck; most such mutations are adverse.

I have argued indeed that, particularly in the case of speculative organizations, the perception of potential threats to survival may be much more important in determining behavior than the perceptions of potential profits, so that profit maximization is not really the driving force. It is fear of loss rather than hope of gain that limits our behavior. So, back to our wheat speculator again; if he is absolutely sure that the price of wheat is going to rise the next day, in the interest of profit maximization he will convert all his resources into wheat, sell everything he has, raise as many loans as he can, go into debt, and acquire the maximum amount of wheat which his resources, the law, and the market permit, assuming here for the moment that there are no transaction costs. The more wheat he possesses today, the more profit he will make when the price rises tomorrow. He is never quite certain, however, that the price is actually going to rise. Suppose it actually falls tomorrow. Then, if he obeyed the profit maximization price criterion, he could very well be wiped out and would not survive. If he could not pay his debts, his net worth might become negative and he would go out of business. Even if he is pretty sure that the price will rise tomorrow, therefore, he will not go all out for wheat; he will retain some liquid assets—he will not sell his house, he will not borrow too much, he will preserve an asset structure—that is, a homeostatic state—which will enable him to survive even if things go very badly.

Redundancy and Adaptability

We see this principle again in the biological world, where redundancy, and even inefficiency, have very important survival value. The efficient species that really maximizes its biological profit, however that is measured, will expand to the full limit of its niche. Then when conditions worsen and the niche shrinks, as in the course of time it eventually will, the species may lack adaptability and have no redundancy to fall back on, and could easily become extinct. This is certainly why in the biosphere there seems to be an enormous amount of redundant behavior. We see the same thing in the economy, in firms and households—in holding reserves, keeping liquid, not committing themselves to too much, going in for assets that are adaptable rather than efficient, and being prepared for large changes in the position of homeostatic equilibrium. Firms, churches, and nations survive by being adaptable. If the market for what they are producing diminishes, they go into something else.

I have heard of one firm that started in domestic laundry equipment, went into automobiles, and ended up by producing beer. This kind of behavior is pretty hard to explain with the marginal analysis. This does not mean, however, that the marginal analysis is useless. It has a value in interpreting homeostatic behavior. Once the homeostatic state itself is chosen, it is by no means unreasonable to suppose that, corresponding to a decision about what product to produce and its image of how to produce it, the firm will select inputs and produce outputs in those quantities which it thinks will maximize some measure of profit. Even the shift from one homeostatic position to another is by no means unconnected with perceptions of greater or lesser overall advantage—that is, with "maximizing utility."

The Equimarginal Principle

There is a useful general theorem (the "equimarginal principle") that in decisions about any kind of distribution of a fixed resource, whether this is the canvas of the painter, the income of the household, or the revenue of the firm, the equimarginal principle applies—that the marginal product, in terms of the maximand, per additional unit of resource in each use should be equal. If shifting the resources from use A to use B gives us a greater gain from B than the loss from A, we will do it; hence we will continue to shift resources until shifting it from A to B would make the loss in A exactly equal to the gain in B, and then we would no longer do it. On the other hand, this assumes knowledge about the effects of our actions, or ar least some image of these effects. These images may be unrealistic and they are subject to constant change in the light of disappointment and further information. Thus, the manner in which past information-input generates expectations of the future is critical in understanding the dynamics of behavior. Yet we have to go well beyond the structure of marginal analysis in order to get at this problem.

Maximizing Profit as a Condition of Survival

Professor Alchian[17] has argued that even though the information structure may not permit firms to maximize profits in fact, simply because of ignorance and the unrealism of their images of the future, there is a selective process which selects for survival those firms which do succeed, partly by chance, in maximizing profits or get close to it, and eliminates those firms which do not. This, of course, is a highly evolutionary perspective, and there is something in it. It is particularly important under conditions approaching perfect competition, in which even equilibrium profits are supposed to be only just about enough to keep the firm alive, and that any shortfall is likely to lead to rapid bankruptcy and disappearance. Certain industries have approximated this condition, such as the early textile industry, with very large numbers of firms and also a very large turnover, with those unfortunate firms which did not maximize their profits simply disappearing and new firms continually coming in in the hope of survival.

Instability of Perfect Competition

This is one reason, however, why perfect competition itself seems to have been somewhat unstable. There may be some biological equivalent of this process in those periods of evolution which have followed some great catastrophe; when the field, as it were, has been wide open, there have been innumerable niches, large rates of mutation, and an enormous turnover of species. Under these circumstances it seems likely that efficiency did pay off and that redundancy and inefficiency led to extinction, simply because of the enormous rate of mutation and the great number of new species coming into the ecosystem all the time. As the ecosystem matures, however, and approaches a more climactic stage, the turnover of species seems to diminish and redundancy seems to develop. In economic life this may correspond to the development of imperfect competition, larger-scale organization, market intervention through selling costs, and even the development of communist states in which there is a single, superdominant species in the shape of government and everything else has shelter under its thorny branches.

The "Colonizing" Versus the "Equilibrium" Modes

Ecological interaction or selection follows rather different patterns in what has been called the "colonizing mode," in which organisms are expanding into a new and unutilized or underutilized environment, and an "equilibrium mode," in which there are no new environments and everything settles down into at least an ecological quasi-equilibrium. In the colonizing mode, selection favors mobility, often increased size, efficiency, active competition, and so on. Many new niches are opening, which means that there are payoffs for a high rate of mutation and adaptability. In an equilibrium mode, mutations are fewer, or at least fewer are likely to succeed. The payoffs are for adaptation, probably some small, high risk-aversion adaptation to rather than an escape from an existing environment, and so on. We see the same phenomenon in social systems. In the last 200 or 300 years, largely because of what may have been an accident that science developed first in Europe, European cultures expanded over the rest of the world to the American continent, to Australasia, South Africa, and so on, and the colonizing mode has been highly dominant. Colonizers tend to increase in size, perhaps in aggressiveness, in competitiveness, in adaptability, in willingness to take risks, in ingenuity, and so on. By comparison, we still have parts of the world in which the equilibrium mode predominates, especially in South and East Asia. Here smaller persons, small-scale operations, highly conservative cultures that transmit themselves almost unchanged from one generation to the next, strong risk aversion, and extremely complex structures of legitimation, have dominated the system for perhaps 3000 years. The incursions of a science-based, colonizing culture into these societies, through corporations, revolutionary governments, universities, the press, radio, and so on, has upset this old equilibrium and has fostered a very sharp rise in population, which has created something like a colonizing culture, at least in the cities. All colonizing cultures, however, eventually come up against the filling up of the new environments and the exhaustion of resources, and almost have to turn again into equilibrium cultures unless new resources and environments are discovered. Thus, the free competition beloved of economists may be a transient phenomenon of colonizing cultures, to be severely modified as colonization reaches its almost inevitable end.

Imperfect Competition as the Learning of Symbiosis

The theory of oligopoly and imperfect competition which has developed in the last fifty years has some important implications for evolutionary economics. Imperfection in competition may develop because of "noogenetic" evolution—that is, a learning process by which there is greater awareness of the ultimate consequences of certain lines of behavior—which may in turn lead to the development of cooperative behavior designed to increase the probability of survival of the existing class of organizations and species. Here again, there may be parallels to this in the biosphere. The development of symbiotic complexes of species seems to be extremely important in survival at certain stages of the process. This symbiosis may, of course, threaten species which do not participate in it, and mutations which lead into such participation may have important survival value. The largest example of this, of course, is the great symbiosis between plants and animals, which undoubtedly expanded very substantially the carrying capacity of the earth in regard to the biosphere. All ecosystems are a mixture of competitive, cooperative, and predative relationships. There may be a drift in the whole evolutionary process toward cooperative complexes, even including predation, for predation is ecologically an unconscious, perhaps rather disagreeable form of cooperation, where both the predator and the predatee help to create a niche for the other.

The Principle of Optimum Variety

A very interesting but rather unsettled question in evolutionary theory, both biological and societal, is that of the optimum degree of variety in an ecosystem. Variety is a kind of insurance against the extinction of the evolutionary process itself. Certainly if terrestrial evolution had produced only one great dragon with his tail curled around the earth, it would have died and that would have been the end of it. As it is, ecosystems are remarkably tough; they can survive all sorts of catastrophes and still continue the evolutionary process, simply because of the enormous variety involved in them. Variety seems to be related to energy throughput and perhaps richness in the material environment. Thus, we go from the 3000 varieties of trees in the tropical forest to the uniform birch forests of the north that border on the tundra, so that latitude is very closely related to the number of species in the prevailing ecosystems. One observes somewhat the same phenomenon in terms of political climate. Societies with a harsh political climate, like Spain of the Inquisition, or the later Islamic Caliphs, or the communist countries today, have a much smaller number of social species, whether commodities, organizations, political parties, churches, or even varieties of persons than do societies where the political climate is warm, genial, tolerant, and does not insist on uniformity. What this says for the survival value of these various types of societies is a complex issue. Certainly societies which have great variety are more likely to survive catastrophe, but they also may generate within themselves climates of moral legitimacy and political belief which are destructive to the very variety which engenders them. Freedom may produce the freedom to destroy freedom, tolerance may tolerate those who will destroy tolerance. Fortunately, this is not always the case, but it is not hard to find examples of this phenomenon in human history. Of course, an intolerance may become intolerable, as we have seen in China and indeed in many societies, so that we seem to have a kind of cyclical movement in this respect.

Macroeconomics: Money as a Unique Product of Evolution of the Economy

The relation of the evolutionary perspective to the development of "macroeconomics," as it began to emerge in the models of Irving Fisher and Knut Wicksell, culminating in John Maynard Keynes, is a little tenuous. Phenomena such as inflation, deflation, and involuntary unemployment have little or no counterpart in biological evolution and in biological ecosystems, mainly because in biological systems there is no equivalent of money—that is, of the generalized medium of exchange and measure of value. There is, as we have seen, something like exchange in the biosphere; for instance, in the metabolism of the organism and in the kind of symbiosis by which the output of one organism becomes the input of another. There is even something a little like circulation in the carbon, nitrogen, and phosphorous cycles. In the biosphere, however, we could say that all exchange is unconscious barter. There is no bargaining, and no generalized medium of exchange.

The introduction of a medium of exchange, therefore, introduces a potential in societal evolution which has no precedent in biological evolution. There is nothing surprising in this. Evolution itself evolves. Money, and the phenomena associated with it, is essentially a part of noogenetic evolution. Money is an image or belief in people's minds, produced by a learning process—we have indeed to learn what is money and what is not—and a system of this kind has properties which transcend the simpler systems of biological interaction and biogenetic evolution.

Money Evolves From Commodity to Symbol

We can see money evolving in the human learning process, beginning with some physical commodity which is very widespread in its ownership, is constantly being exchanged, and which therefore people learn to accept not for its own sake but because it can be exchanged for something else. A great variety of commodities have occupied this role—

cattle (the word pecuniary comes from the Latin "pecus" meaning cattle), iron and iron articles, then of course the precious metals such as gold and silver. These turned out to be highly suitable for occupying what might be called the monetary niche. They are sufficiently scarce and in sufficiently general use so that their price per unit of weight is fairly high, and one can transport purchasing power fairly easily. They are also subdividable, easily recognized, identifiable, and so on.

When the monetary commodity becomes a symbol of value another great step is taken. This can happen even with gold and silver and other commodities because of their visibility. In many cultures riches are displayed in the form of gold and silver adornments. The next step is where the symbol replaces the commodity, as in paper money. This seems to have been done in China many centuries ago. Paper money, or symbolic money, orginates in the form of a promise to deliver a commodity or commodity money. If these promises are trusted and believed, they will themselves then become exchangeables and will circulate in the market. This leads into abstract money, like bank deposits, which simply represent a promise on the part of the banker to deliver money up to the amount of the deposit whenever the owner asks for it. This promise becomes so universally believed that it represents an asset to the depositor which he can transfer freely to others, and which hence can circulate as a medium of exchange.

Inflation Potential in Symbolic Money

Once money has become symbolic the possibility of inflation emerges. The first such symbol is the coin, which is supposed to have been invented about 640 B.C. in the Mediterranean, probably earlier in China. With coinage comes the depreciation of the currency by replacing an expensive metal with a cheaper one, thus increasing the total number of coins. If these are still accepted at face value, prices in terms of the currency unit will begin to rise and we have inflation. Deflation may also occur if there is a drain of the metallic money out of the society in response, for instance, to an excess of imports. Both inflation and deflation have redistributive effects. Inflation redistributes real assets away from those who hold money and debt contracts in monetary units and toward those who hold real commodities and things which are rising in price, and their symbols such as shares of stock. Deflation redistributes real assets the other way, toward the money and debt holders, away from the holders of real assets.

As it tends to be the holders of real assets that make the essential decisions about their allocation and utilization, inflation may encourage the accumulation and productive use of real assets, while deflation may have the opposite effect. Uncertainty and insecurity likewise have profound effects on the willingness to hold, acccumulate, organize, and allocate real assets. In times of extreme insecurity, there is a tendency to transfer real assets, for instance, into monetary hoards which are easy to protect, so that the fields go untilled, workshops are neglected, and houses fall to ruin. Even before the development of complex and active labor markets, therefore, there is some evidence for overall impacts of deflation or inflation on the general development of society, and its movement from riches into poverty or poverty into riches.

Unemployment

With the decline and eventual abolition of slavery and serfdom, and an increase in the proportion of the active labor force obtaining employment in free labor markets, another phenomenon begins to emerge, which is involuntary unemployment. Employment is an exchange, though a rather complex one, between an employer who offers a wage, usually in the form of money but occasionally in kind, to the worker in return for the worker obeying the instructions of the employer or his representative in regard to a certain period of activity in time. This exchange is unlikely to take place unless the alternatives to both parties are perceived to be less favorable. In the case of the employer, giving employment (it is interesting that we use the word "giving" in this connection) involves giving up the wage, usually in the form of money, in return for the product of the work, which will be realized sometime in the future. Unless the value of the product of the work in the mind of the employer is greater than the value of the wage, the bargain will not be struck. If the money which would be paid out in the wage can be put out at interest, then unless the rate of expected profit in the labor bargain—that is, the rate of growth of the value of capital employed in the form of the product of the labor—is greater than the rate of interest by an amount sufficient to compensate for the risks and uncertainties, the labor bargain will not be struck, the worker will not be employed, the employer will hold his assets in the form of interest bearing loans, and we may get involuntary unemployment.

Involuntary unemployment probably begins quite early in human history, though it is not recorded as such until a fairly late date. The plebs of ancient Rome, the sturdy beggars of Elizabethan England all suggest that this is a fairly ancient phenomenon. Not until the collection of social information begins to include unemployment statistics, however, does this become clearly visible and important as an object of policy. In the twentieth century it has become extremely noticeable. In the Great Depression of the early 1930s, for instance, unemployment was almost 25 percent in the United States; that is, a quarter of the labor force at the then existing wage structure would have liked to have had a job and could not find one.

The Keynesian Revolution

The Keynesian revolution in economic thought[18] is fairly complex, but it has two main pillars, one concerned with the monetary aspects of the economy, the other with "real" aspects, in terms of real goods. The monetary aspect relates to the impact of deflation or inflation on the difference between the interest on loans and profit on real assets. Real interest rates are roughly equal to nominal interest rates minus the rate of inflation or plus the rate of deflation. Suppose, for instance, I borrow $100 at 5 percent, so I contract to pay back $105 in one year's time. If in that interval there has been a 3 percent inflation, the $105 in a year's time only represents $102 of the earlier price level. The real rate of interest is only 2 percent. If there has been a 3 percent deflation, the $105 a year from now is worth $108 of this year, and the real rate of interest is 8 percent. Where inflations or deflations are not anticipated, or where they take place rather suddenly, nominal interest rates cannot adjust to them. Deflation, therefore, increases real interest rates; inflation diminishes them.

Inflation and deflation, however, also have an impact on profits. Profits are made by buying something at one time and selling it at a higher price later. If in the interval all prices have risen in an inflation, the chance of increasing profits is high. If in the interval all prices have fallen, the chance of profits is lower. From both sides, therefore, an unanticipated deflation diminishes the gap between interest and profit; an unanticipated inflation increases the gap. It is not surprising that deflation is associated with large unemployment and inflation with small unemployment.

The "real goods" leg of the Keynesian revolution begins from a simple identity, that the rate of accumulation of real goods is equal to their rate of production minus their rate of consumption. Another way of stating this is to say that everything that has been produced in a given period has either been consumed, or is still around. In any given state of society there is some rate of accumulation of real goods which is "acceptable," in the sense that it will not produce inflation, deflation or unemployment. If the gap between production and consumption rises above this, so that there is an "unacceptable" increase in the stock of real goods, the owners of these will try to unload them, with the result that the price level will fall, that is, there will be some deflation with the adverse effects noted above. With a rise in unemployment, production will decline, but consumption will decline also because of the falling incomes, so that there still may be a rate of accumulation that is unacceptable, further deflation, further unemployment, and so on, until the falling consumption begins to flatten out as we get close to basic necessities, the gap between production and consumption closes, and accumulation sinks to what is acceptable, though what is acceptable may itself by this time have shrunk. This is the "underemployment equilibrium."

The existence of financial markets and speculative movements in these markets again complicates the picture. The collapse of a speculative stock market boom, as in 1929, may set off a period of low investment and business timidity. There are also significant movements in the relative commodity price and wage structure during inflation and deflation which arise out of the fact that some prices and wages react to a general inflationary or deflationary movement much more rapidly than others. Hence, there are dynamically produced distortions in the relative price structure which may have serious consequences.

Economic Cycles

Overall movements of deflation, inflation, and unemployment frequently exhibit a cyclical pattern, or at least a pattern of irregular fluctuations. There are two kinds of systems which exhibit cyclical or fluctuating patterns. One is an essentially equilibrium system, like a pendulum, in which the movement towards equilibrium overshoots and goes past the equilibrium point, has to return to it, overshoots it again, and so on. The other pattern is like that of a ball bouncing between the hand and the floor, in which an ongoing, and perhaps self-generating, dynamic movement is suddenly reversed at a boundary. The first kind of system depends on negative feedback; the second depends on positive feedback—with what might be called "reversing boundaries." In a system with negative feedback, of which the thermostat is a good example, there is some equilibrium position of the system, for instance, the temperature at which the thermostat is set. If the equilibrium variable rises above this, apparatus of some kind is brought into play to lower it. If the equilibrium falls below this, apparatus is brought into play to raise it. Cycles may be set up, because as the system moves toward the equilibrium it develops a certain momentum of its own which carries it past the equilibrium, but when it goes far enough past the equilibrium, the system itself reverses the process and brings it back again, but again may overshoot. The amplitude of these negative feedback cycles depends on the sensitivity of the system to the information that it is not in equilibrium. Positive feedback systems have a different pattern. If we had a thermostat in which when the temperature got "high" the furnace turned on, when the temperature got "low" it turned off, we would have a positive feedback system with extreme fluctuations. In some cases, this can lead to the destruction of the system itself, unless there are reversing boundaries which the system hits and reverses its direction of motion.

Economic cycles can have characteristics of both these systems. In purely speculative markets, for instance, there are cycles which somewhat resemble the pendulum. Suppose we start, for instance, at the point where stock prices are perceived as "low." There will be an increased demand for stocks, a diminished demand for money, orders to buy will exceed orders to sell, and the price will rise. As it rises, this may engender a belief that the price will go on rising, through what might be called a "trend expectation," which easily turns into a trend fallacy. Prices cannot rise, however, without becoming high; and when they become high, there is increasing belief that they will fall. As this belief gathers strength, selling orders will exceed buying orders, and prices will begin to fall. This reinforces the belief that they will fall, and they fall still further. As they go on falling, however, they eventually become "low," and the cycle starts all over again. Sometimes the turning points are very dramatic, especially on the downward side, and involve a "crash" like that of 1929.

Employment cycles tend to be more of the "bouncing ball" variety. The Keynesian dynamic of diminished employment leading to declining incomes, further unwanted accumulations, more unemployment, more declining incomes, and so on, could continue until it hits some kind of a bottom boundary, at which the "propensity to consume" suddenly changes. This may start the system bouncing up again, until it reaches some kind of upper boundary toward full employment. The decline in the amplitude of economic cycles in the past fifty years may be due either to greater sensitivity in feedback information, as perhaps has happened with inventory cycles, or to a narrowing of the range within which the ball is bouncing, as perhaps has happened with unemployment.

The Great Depression

The Great Depression of the 1930s was a good example of these principles. It began with the speculative stock market boom and crash of 1929. This led to pessimism in the business community and declining investment, or a declining willingness to accept increase in capital stocks. This led to repayment of bank loans, a decline in bank deposits, and a banking deflation. These processes were not offset by any rise in government expenditure to correspond, nor by any rise in consumption, which itself was declining. The deflation and decline in investment fed on itself in a positive feedback process, until by 1932-1933 the national income in money terms was almost half that of 1929, corporate profits were negative, unemployment was 25 percent, and the banking system had virtually collapsed. Distortions in the relative price structure were severe. In agriculture prices were highly flexible, so that with the halving of the money value of the national income, agricultural prices about halved but agricultural output stayed up. The halving of the national money income was reflected fairly evenly in the different sectors of the economy, in all of which income about halved. In agriculture this happened because of the halving of prices. In large parts of the industrial sector prices only fell about 25 percent, and output and employment fell about 25 percent because of the "stickiness" of industrial wages and prices.

The federal government was such a small part of the economy in those days that, even if it had tried to offset the movement, it would probably not have had the capability. Understanding of the system was so imperfect, however, that President Hoover actually sponsored a tax increase in 1932, which unquestionably intensified the depression. Then from 1933 on, depreciation of capital in the previous four years almost forced an increase in investment. The New Deal exercised a very small inflationary pressure. Most of the recovery from 1932 to 1937 was spontaneous in the private sector. Then in 1938 the introduction of Social Security created a sharp deflationary movement, because of increased net taxes, with a very sharp depression in 1938. Then, World War II came along and the enormous rise in government expenditures virtually eliminated unemployment by 1940 or 1941.

The "Long Boom"

The extraordinary stability of the American economy from 1950 on—which might almost be called the "long boom"—may be attributed to the stability of business investment. Just why this has been so stable is not altogether clear. In the last forty years, there has been a substantial improvement in the information system of the economy with the development of national income statistics. There has been an improvement, also, in the policy-making process, with the development of the Council of Economic Advisors in the office of the President, and the Joint Economic Committee in Congress. If we had had this knowledge and these institutions in 1929, we would undoubtedly have been able to avoid a depression of such unprecedented severity.

What we now seem to be unable to avoid is inflation, for the financial system has now (1981) adjusted to the rate of inflation. Nominal interest rates have risen to the point where real interest rates are now perhaps even too high, for the rise in interest has created a squeeze in profits as a proportion of national income. Under these circumstances, a sudden cessation of the inflation could well be catastrophic, simply because we could probably not adjust nominal interest rates fast enough, and we would run into the old problem of the gap between interest and profit being too small to make the employment of the unemployed profitable. The great difficulty here is that interest contracts have a great variety of period of maturity and very little flexibility. At the present time sudden cessation of the inflation would put an intolerable burden on the holders of mortgages, at say 13 percent. As long as the inflation is held at 10 percent per annum, 13 percent interest, as we have seen, is only 3 percent in real terms, which is bearable. With no inflation we would have a real rate of interest of 13 percent, which would be intolerable. Short-term debt, of course, can easily be refinanced at lower rates of interest, but this is difficult to do with long-term debt. We might even have to adopt a Draconian policy of rendering all existing contracts invalid, only validating them if the rate of interest in all of them is halved. The problem here is one of redistribution over people who have made different commitments at different times. This is an extremely difficult problem in social justice.

Our inability to devise institutions which will stop the inflation, however, lands us in an even greater danger, which is that of accelerating inflation. Constant inflation at a fairly low rate, of the sort that we had in the 1950s and 1960s, is not much of a burden on a society. It will involve some redistributions, on the whole away from those who did not anticipate it toward those who did, whether consciously or accidentally. The effects, however, are fairly small, as long as the constant rate of inflation does not exceed, say, 3 or 5 percent per annum. An accelerating inflation, however, such as we have been experiencing in the 1970s, cannot continue for very long, or it will end up in hyperinflation, which is very destructive. This involves a total collapse of the value of money, the sort of thing that happened in Germany in 1923 or in Hungary after World War II. This always has to be followed by drastic currency reform and involves very large redistributions among individuals. It also produces hoarding of goods, and increasing unemployment as markets become more and more disorganized and impossible to predict.

The Phillips' Curve Dilemma

The dilemma of inflation and unemployment is often called the "Phillips' curve dilemma" from a famous curve drawn by A. W. Phillips.[19] In the usual way in which the curve is presented today—a downward sloping line with unemployment on one axis and inflation on the other— (Phillips himself used money wages)—it is supposed to show that we can only purchase lower unemployment with higher inflation. There may be two general reasons for the existence of this relationship. One, particularly associated with the name of Keynes, is called the "bottleneck problem." As the money stock is increased, money demands tend to increase. If supply curves are elastic, as they are likely to be if there is large-scale unemployment and unutilized capacity, it is very easy to expand output. An increase in demand will mainly be felt in increased employment and output, not in prices. At some point, however, in one industry after another, supplies become less elastic, easily available capacity of plant is reached, increased demand for labor starts to push up money wages, and we begin to get inflation.

A second possible factor in the relationship is, as we have seen, that inflation tends to push distribution away from interest towards profits, and this is likely to increase the demand for labor and lessen unemployment unless it is offset by rising wages. The interaction among wages and prices is extraordinarily complex and hard to predict and the data in this area is very poor.

In accelerating inflation, the Phillips' curve seems to be pushed continually upward, so that a given level of unemployment requires a continually higher rate of inflation to sustain it. This may happen if interest rates adjust too readily to the inflation, as inflation then no longer performs the function of redistributing income away from interest towards profits. This seems to have been happening in the United States in the 1970s.

Intervention in Financial Markets

Without intervention into the financial markets on a scale for which there is little precedent or skill, it is ominously hard to see how accelerating inflation can be avoided. Up to now we have assumed that all the intervention that was necessary in the financial markets was through agents like the Federal Reserve System, with a little qualitative regulation by the Securities and Exchange Commission. The Federal Reserve system intervenes partly by regulation—for instance, of bank reserve ratios—but mainly in these days by open market operations, by which it hopes to expand or contract the total money stock. The reserves of member banks consist mainly of Federal Reserve Bank deposits and the Federal Reserve system can expand these by purchasing securities with deposits which it creates, and can contract these by selling securities and using the proceeds to purchase its own deposits held outside the banks or elsewhere. This will reduce bank reserves, which may force a reduction of bank deposits on the part of the money stock in the private sector. There has been very little intervention, however, in the terms of existing contracts, though there is a certain precedent in the abrogation of the gold clause in the early days of the New Deal. Many contracts at that time had a clause which stated that the payments were to be made in the dollar value of so many ounces of gold, and the law simply abrogated those clauses, illustrating indeed a very fundamental principle that even private contracts are essentially creatures of the law and therefore of the state.

Inflation in an Evolutionary Perspective

Applying the perspective of evolutionary economics to these problems, we can put the question of inflation in the form, "Why does the niche for the number of dollars in the total money stock of a society continually increase?" If the money stock is a commodity money, like gold or silver, the increase in the stock can only come through an excess of production from mining or net import over consumption through abrasion and loss, or perhaps withdrawal into other uses, like plate or jewelry, plus net exports. As soon as money becomes a symbol, however, there are very few physical obstacles to its continual production. Increasing the money stock physically simply involves printing more bills or writing more numbers in bank ledgers, or even in bank computers. The question then arises, "What under these circumstances limits the 'birth' of new units of money stock, new dollars?" The answer is that money stock increases by a complex of decisions, particularly on the part of the officials of government and central bankers and commercial bankers. These decisions are then made in the light of some standard of failure or success, particularly in regard to other variables of the economy.

The situation is complicated by political decisions about the size of the budget deficits or surpluses. A cash deficit means that the government is paying out more than it is taking in, in some form of money, which will increase the money stocks in the hands of the people. An unwillingness to raise taxes in the face of expanding expenditures, is particularly noticeable in time of war, and is an important causal factor in expanding the money stock through the budget deficit. A cash deficit is not quite the same thing as fiscal deficit, which may be partly financed by the issue of securities to the public rather than cash, but the relationship is fairly close. The motivations behind deficits are complex and may have something to do with the political unacceptability of raising taxes, political demands for new programs of expenditure, or it may be something more subtle, a feeling that the monetary expansion as a result of the deficit is necessary in order to raise the level of employment. This motivation may be particularly noticeable in the months before an election.[20]

There is considerable controversy among economists over the question of what overall decision-making process leads to an increase (or decrease) in the total stock of money or other liquid assets relative to other things. The increase in the money stock is certainly the main driving force towards inflation, as its dimunition is the main drive towards deflation. But what determines the increase or decrease in the stock of money depends on the institutions of the monetary system and is a result of a complex series of interacting decisions on the part of sections of government, central banks, other banks, private investors and capitalists, and so on. The assumption made by the extreme monetarists that the stock of money is determined wholly by the independent and autonomous decisions of the central bank seems to me quite unrealistic. In all countries central banks are strongly subject to pressure from governments, even when they are officially quasi-dependent, as the Federal Reserve System is in the United States. In these days, especially, a government faced with rising unemployment is likely not only to increase its deficits, but also to pressure the central banks and the banking system generally to increase the money stock and so probably diminish unemployment at the cost of inflation.

The evolutionary approach to this problem would also look at both the employed and the unemployed as species each with a niche. We see the niche of the employed created by two characteristics of the system: the willingness of private firms to hire people, very closely related to the expectations of profit or interest as we have seen; and the willingness of government and charitable enterprises to hire people. The interactions among these are complex and hard to spell out, but this is at least a useful way to look at the problem. There is a further niche of the "labor force"—that subset of the population who would like to be employed.

This depends on many factors—the nature of the family, the structure of property income and grants, and so on. The "unemployed" are simply those members of the labor force who are not members of the employed.

Unemployment and Inflation in Centrally Planned Economies

Centrally planned economies have had less unemployment and inflation than the capitalist economies over the last forty years, simply because when the state is almost the sole employer the power of the worker to raise wages is enormously diminished, and the people who make bad decisions about employing people are not the ones who suffer by it. Full employment is, however, bought at the cost of large inefficiencies and exploitations. It is interesting to note also that Yugoslavia, which is the freest communist country in Europe, has had one of the highest rates of inflation in Europe for the last few years, which suggests that it is at least as hard to run a liberal socialist economy as it is to run a capitalist economy in regard to the macroeconomic problems. The Polish strikes of 1980 also suggest that even in a communist state the power of the monopolist state employer is not incapable of erosion.

It is clear that in regard to these macroeconomic problems we are in an evolutionary process far more complex than that of prehuman biological evolution. Nevertheless, it is an evolutionary, and not merely an equilibrium or mechanical process, and our hope of resolving these difficult problems lies in the clear perception of the evolutionary framework in which they lie. No policy can be successful unless it recognizes the constant drift of evolutionary change, as we shall see in the final chapter.

Notes

1. Adam Smith, *The Wealth of Nations* (New York: Random House/Modern Library Edition, 1965).
2. T. R. Malthus, *Population, the First Essay* (Ann Arbor, Michigan: Ann Arbor Paperbacks, 1959).
3. David Ricardo, *On the Principles of Political Economy, and Taxation*, 1817 (New York: Dutton/Everyman's Library, 1969).
4. John Stuart Mill, *Principles of Political Economy*, 1848, 2 vols., edited by J. M. Robson. (Toronto: University of Toronto Press, 1965).
5. Karl Marx, *Capital*, 1867-1879, 3 vols. (Moscow: Progress Publishers, 1965-1966).
6. Charles Darwin, *On the Origin of Species*, 1859 (Cambridge, Mass.: Harvard University Press, 1964).

7. Alfred Marshall, *Principles of Economics*, 1890, 9th ed. (London: Macmillan, 1961).

8. Leon Walras, *Elements of Pure Economics*, 1874, 4th ed. (Homewood, Ill.: Richard D. Irwin, 1954).

9. Paul Samuelson, *Foundations of Economic Analysis* (Cambridge, Mass.: Harvard University Press, 1947).

10. Paul Samuelson, "Unemployment Ahead," *The New Republic* CXI (September 11, 1944), 297-299.

11. Joseph Schumpeter, *The Theory of Economic Development*, 1912 trans. by Redvers Opie (Cambridge, Mass.: Harvard University Press, 1934).

12. Joseph Schumpeter, *Capitalism, Socialism and Democracy* (New York: Harper & Row, 1942).

13. Roy F. Harrod, *Towards a Dynamic Economics* (New York: Macmillan, 1948).

14. Evsey Domar, *Essays in the Theory of Economic Growth* (New York: Oxford University Press, 1957).

15. Almost any standard economics textbook develops these propositions. I have done so myself in K. E. BOULDING, *Economics Analysis*, Vol. 2 (New York: Harper & Row, 1966).

16. The classic description of homeostasis is Walter B. Cannon, *The Wisdom of the Body* (New York: W. W. Norton, 1963).

17. A. A. Alchian, "Uncertainty, Evolution and Economic Theory," *Journal of Political Economy* LVIII (1950).

18. John M. Keynes, *The General Theory of Employment, Interest and Money* (London: Macmillan, 1936).

19. A. W. Phillips, "The Relation Between Unemployment and the Rate of Change of Money Wages in the United Kingdom, 1961-1957," *Economica* N.S. 25 (November 1958), 283-299.

20. Edward R. Tufte, *Political Control of the Economy* (Princeton, N.J.: Princeton University Press, 1978).

CHAPTER 4

The Evolutionary Approach to Economic History

"Provisioning" Versus "Exchangeables" as a Focus of Economic History

Economic history is a somewhat vague subset of the history of the human race. It deals with the production, exchange, consumption, and distribution of human artifacts and also of certain natural objects, such as land, minerals, and water, insofar as these are used by human beings and especially insofar as they are appropriated and become property and participate in exchange relationships. There may be two possible views as to what constitutes the economic section of human life and history; the "provisioning" view and the "exchangeables" view. We may look first at what might be called "provisions;" those natural objects and human artifacts which conduce to the better living of human life and to human "betterment"—that is, to changes in the state of the person and environment which are positively evaluated. Provisions may be developed without exchange, as in the classic example of Robinson Crusoe, who catches fish, collects or grows food, builds a house, makes clothing for himself, and so on, and so changes his near and moderately near environment, in his own valuations, for the better. Here, of course, there are past exchange elements, such as Robinson Crusoe's skills and culture derived from a very complex society in which exchange played a very important part. Nevertheless, it is not unreasonable to suppose that in some sense "provisioning," that is, a valuable change in environment and in the throughput which these environments involve, is in some sense prior to exchange and that exchange must be regarded essentially as a means to the end of better provisioning.

Provisions, however, may include the artifacts of religious, political, military and social life which have an economic aspect but are not thought of as constituting the "economic" part of life. Temples, churches, weapons, defenses, status symbols, and so on are the result of economic activity but are part of certain noneconomic aspects of life. Within the broad field of provisioning, therefore, it is not unreasonable to see exchange as that aspect of life which is most clearly economic and to look at economic history as the study of how the history of the human race has been in part organized by exchange and related activities, such as production and consumption of exchangeables and also the one-way transfer of exchangeables in gifts and grants.

Economic History as a Subset of Human History under Noogenetic Evolution

The evolutionary approach to economic history is a subset of the evolutionary approach to human history as a whole. It starts with Adam and Eve—whatever their names were—the first specimens of Homo sapiens with their extraordinary potential and capacity for knowledge, skill, and the production of artifacts. At the beginning this potential was largely unrealized and unused, which raises, of course, the very tricky question as to how natural selection produced Homo sapiens, especially with an organ such as the brain which apparently was almost entirely redundant in its early stages. That is a question we can leave to one side. We are sure that at some point in the biological evolution of the human race creatures were around that had the capacity of complex images of the world and for language. The history of language has left no record before the advent of writing, so we know very little about it, but it is clear that it gave the human race an extraordinary capacity for expanding its knowledge structure. Language enables us to transmit images from one mind into another without direct experience, so that the individual human being can know an enormous number of things of which there is no direct experience at all. I, for instance, have a fairly clear image in my mind of Gibraltar, which I have never seen, an image derived from descriptions and pictures. Probably not even the brightest chimpanzee could have such an image, although there are signs that the potential of the chimpanzee is larger than we thought, for instance, in regard to language.

Human history is almost entirely the realization of the "noogenetic" potential of the human race for the development of knowledge ("know-what") and skill ("know-how") in the human mind and body. Even in many prehuman species there is a mixture of biogenetic information structures derived from the genes and "noogenetic" structures which are derived from a learning process which is transmitted from one generation to the next. Birds learn at least the details of their song; kittens learn from their mothers, and monkeys learn a great deal of their behavior. In humans noogenetic evolution becomes completely dominant; human genes have changed very little in 50,000 years. I learned the English language from my parents, they learned it from theirs, and theirs from theirs, and so on. It changed somewhat in the process, but retained an enormous complexity of structure from one generation to the next. Our biogenetic structure in the genes gave us the potential for language in the brain, but plays no part in specifying the form, vocabulary, and structure of a language, which is purely noogenetic.

Provisioning is something which goes back a long way in the evolution of life. Squirrels gather nuts, birds build nests, beavers build dams, and so on. Virtually all of these skills, however, are biogenetic in origin, that is, "instinct." There are some exceptions to this in prehuman organisms—baby beavers may learn something about dams and baby monkeys develop a good deal of noogenetic culture and behavior which is transmitted from one generation to the next after some genius has invented it. In the human race, however, noogenetic transmission is completely dominant. There has been very little biogenetic change in humans since their species began. Biogenetic differences in human beings, while they are important from one individual to the next, do not seem to be important over moderately large groups. Racial differences are, of course, a result of biogenetic differences, but these tend to be very superficial—minor matters like skin or eye color or hair color and texture—and have very little relevance to noogenetic potential, which seems to be very equally and widely distributed throughout the whole race.

Periods of Human History

(1) Paleolithic

The history of the human race is usually divided into three main periods: (1) the paleolithic "old stone age" (characterized by artifacts of stone and wood, with the food supply provided essentially by hunting and gathering);[1] (2) the neolithic "new stone age," in which comes the development of agriculture and the domestication of livestock; and (3) the movement into civilization involving metallurgy, moving from copper and gold and silver to bronze, to iron and steel, and to the development of large-scale organizations and cities. Throughout the whole history of the human race there is constant change in knowledge and artifacts, although in the earlier periods this change seems almost inconceivably slow for those of us who are familiar with the modern world. It is hard for us to imagine indeed how beings genetically virtually identical with ourselves could have gone through hundreds of generations with very little change in the flint knives and arrowheads and the other durable artifacts which have come down to us. One suspects that there was greater change in the nondurable artifacts that did not survive—things such as language, family patterns, ritual; and perhaps perishable artifacts—wood, skins, and so on. All this is lost to us.

The only explanation I can think of for this cultural stability in the paleolithic period is that the length of life was so short and conditions so harsh that it took almost all of the teaching capacity of one generation to transmit the existing structure of knowledge to the next, so that there was very little time or energy left over for innovation and for new learning. There seem to have been brief periods of advance represented, for instance, by the cave paintings of France. But where the human group was probably not more than 50 or 100 at most, a cumulative learning process might take place for four or five generations and then some accident or sudden worsening of conditions, like war with a neighboring group or an epidemic would kill off all of the older people of the group who knew anything before they could transmit this knowledge to the young, and the group would fall back to the level of some generations before. This agonizing process of alternating development and collapse must have gone on for many thousands of years.

(2) Neolithic

With the invention of agriculture there is evidence that the average age of death rose from perhaps thirty to forty because of the improved food supply, better housing, and clothing. This set up an irreversible process of expansion in human knowledge. It was now possible not only to transmit knowledge structure from one generation to the next but to have a little time to increase it. It is not surprising therefore, that with agriculture comes metallurgy, pottery, weaving, stone houses, more travel and trade, astronomy, Stonehenge and Carnac, the beginnings of monumental structures, and finally civilization—that is, cities drawing their food from a surrounding countryside, in the first instance almost certainly through some kind of organized threat system, whether spiritual in the case of the temple, or material in the case of kings and armies.

(3) Civilization

There is some evidence of a reduction in the average age at death in the new cities, but they also produced a leisure class who were able to specialize in knowledge. So we get the very early beginnings of science in Babylon, India, China, Greece, and in Mesoamerica. For the first 2000 years science developed sporadically and was constantly threatened by war and the destruction of the cities where it flourished, or even from their attrition and decay. We do not know, of course, how much was lost in this period, and a surprising amount was transmitted precariously from one center to another—from Thebes to Babylon, to Athens, to Alexandria, to Rome, to Bagdad, perhaps to Delhi and to Changan and Peking, as cities rose and fell. From about 1500 on, however, science developed as a continuing subculture in Europe with a cumulative growth of human knowledge from one generation to the next. The growth indeed accelerated steadily. There seems to be a point where the greater the stock of knowledge the easier it is to acquire more. We begin to know how to increase knowledge. The scientific revolution indeed was precisely that—a change in the way in which knowledge was increased.

Writing and Records

The prosthetic devices by which knowledge is stored, organized, and transmitted outside of direct person-to-person contact, again, grow

almost exponentially. From the beginnings of civilization, writing, government, and cities go hand in hand. Without records the continuity of
organizations from one generation to the next cannot be maintained
and communications cannot be transmitted from the decision-making
center to the acting periphery. Writing seems to begin with some kind of
organizational accounting and inventory, as in Knossos. Soon this
flowers into written poetry, literature and drama, which had existed
precariously a long time before in oral forms. With writing comes the
possibility of communication from the dead, even the long dead, to the
living. This enormously expands the time dimension of the communication and learning process. This removed the limitations on the growth
of human knowledge which were set in a preliterature age by the fact
that only a very small number of people could communicate with each
other, and then only for the most part the living to the living. The total
body of human knowledge potentially accessible to an individual grew
constantly, as each generation left its deposit of writing.

Science and Post-Civilization

It was no accident that science comes along with printing, which again
enormously increases the number of people who can be at least in one-
way communication. Something may be lost qualitatively by the decline
in conversation—that is, two-way exchange of information as a component of knowledge formation; for instance, I could never have a
debate with Adam Smith or Marx. The quantitative increase in
communication, however, is so large it apparently more than counter-
balances any qualitative loss. With the rise of organized science, it could
be argued that a fourth stage in human development, which has been
called "post-civilization," begins to get under way with a science-based
technology. This, indeed, is where the developed world is today, while
the poor countries are still in the stage of classical civilization. The
neolithic and paleolithic cultures have virtually disappeared, except for a
few isolated and rapidly diminishing cases.

Economic Development and the Evolutionary Model

Human history follows the broad patterns of the evolution of life itself.
We perceive in economic history, and indeed in the whole history of the
human race, a process that seems to have a "time's arrow"; something

that can legitimately be called "growth"; in economic history, "economic growth." There are, of course, ups and downs, periods of retrogression in particular places, though rarely for the world as a whole. There seems to be a persistent bias, however, toward increase in "riches"—that is, in the number, complexity, and capacity of human artifacts with which we are surrounded. It is a long way from the first appearance of Homo sapiens, living perhaps in caves, using primitive wood or stone implements, perhaps not even having fire, or skins for clothing, to the life of the average citizen in the developed countries today living in a house or apartment surrounded by hundreds of different artifacts—furniture, clothing, books, pictures, china, electric light, appliances, and so on— usually having an automobile or at least a bicycle, able to read, having some peculiar skills of a trade or profession, aware of a good deal of what goes on in the world, often politically active, and so on. Economic history is part of the process that leads from the first state to the second and it is not surprising that we think of it in terms of "development," even recognizing that all growth is not development and all development may not be for the good.

What light, then, does the evolutionary model shed on this vast process of economic development as it stretches out over space and time? It is not a mechanical model like celestial mechanics, which can enable us to perceive a single, deterministic pattern of the past and project this into the future. It is a model which recognizes the importance of randomness; the possibility that what actually happened is a partially accidental subset of what might have happened. Nevertheless, the evolutionary model does enable us to perceive certain kinds of order in this pattern and to achieve greater understanding of how it proceeds through time.

Evolution as the Filling of "Empty Niches"

Three major concepts are important here: one is the concept of the "empty niche" in some kind of ecosystem, defined as a species which does not presently exist in the system, but which if it did exist would have an equilibrium population. Empty niches are created and destroyed all the time as changes take place in the rest of the system. There was clearly an empty niche for the human race some 50,000 to 100,000 years ago, which there certainly would not have been a billion years earlier, before the development of plants and animals that served for human food. As soon as humans appeared, the niche structure of the ecosystems into which they penetrated began to change quite rapidly. The niche for Neanderthal humans closed, and they became extinct. Humans opened a niche for domesticated animals, with the dog perhaps being the first, which, however, was not filled for many thousands of years in some cases.

Crises and the "Threshold Effect"

There is a phenomenon here which might be called a "potential niche," which is hard to get into because the population which would occupy it is only viable beyond a certain size and hence it may be difficult for it to grow to this size. As long as it is below the viable size, even if it starts to enter the system it will tend to decline and become extinct. In the paleolithic period, for instance, it is likely that many inventions were not made which would have been very useful simply because there would be strong resistance to anything that was novel. In a world where human life itself is highly precarious, any innovation might be seen as a threat. This, again, perhaps, explains why the culture and artifacts of the paleolithic were so extraordinarily stable for such a long period. This might be called a "threshold effect," that an innovation has to gather a certain amount of momentum to reach a certain size before it gets over the threshold into the niche that is waiting for it.

Sometimes indeed a dramatic worsening of the situation may push potential innovations over the niche threshold. It has been argued, for instance, that the last ice age pushed the human race down into the narrower peninsulas of the world, in the northern hemisphere at least—for instance, Mexico, Spain, Italy, Greece, Mesopotamia, India, South Asia—and created a sufficient sense of crisis and also congestion so that agriculture developed. It is puzzling indeed why agriculture was not invented 20,000 years before. We certainly had the wit to do it. This may be an example of the famous principle that only necessity is the mother of invention. Curiosity may be the father, but fathers without mothers produce no offspring! If it had not been for the strain created by the ice age, the human race might have continued on its hunting and gathering way with little incentive to change or to learn. The idea of collecting seeds to plant seems so obvious it is hard to believe that it was not done many times, but perhaps there had to be a sense of dire necessity before it became universal.

Agriculture, Domestication, and Boats

In any case, agriculture led to a profound change in the whole way of life of humankind. A settled agriculture opened up innumerable new niches—in the first place for villages, for adequate permanent housing did not have to be transported. The domestication of livestock may well have begun with the hunters and gatherers, turning them into nomadic herdsmen, which is a kind of halfway house towards agriculture, providing a permanent source of food on the hoof instead of in the field. The domestication of riding animals, like the horse, donkey, or camel, may well have preceded agriculture and even helped to open up the niche for it. Agriculture, however, often seems to have gone hand in hand with the domestication of some kind of draft animal, whether the horse, donkey, water buffalo or llama. These considerably increased human productivity in the production of food and in the ability to transport both human beings and their goods over distances. Boats may have come almost at the same time, although possibly 2000 or 3000 years later. The development of water transportation on large rivers, such as the Nile, the Indus, and the Huang-Ho may have opened a niche for the first civilizations in those areas.

The Role of Energy and Materials as Limits

A very important principle is at work here in explaining how empty niches get filled. This is the evolutionary view of the process of production. The evolutionary model sees production as a process by which the genotype becomes the phenotype, how, for instance, an egg becomes a chicken and an idea in somebody's head becomes a human artifact. A process of production always originates in the genotype, that is, with some kind of know-how which is capable of planning and organizing the process. This genetic information structure, however, always has to be able to capture energy, for instance, chemical energy in the yolk or the white in the case of the egg, from the mother's blood-stream in the case of the mammal, and from the energy inputs of the economic system in the case of the human artifact. With this energy the genetic structure transmits information, sustains appropriate temperatures, and does work, that is, transports, rearranges, and transforms material into the improbable shapes of the phenotype or artifact. Energy and materials are the limiting factors of this process. In the absence of sufficient energy, the right kind of materials or the right places, all the genetic know-how in the world will not enable its potential to be realized.

A very significant fact of evolution, however, is that as the genetic know-how structure develops and becomes increasingly complex the increase of know-how itself tends to push back the energy and materials' limitations and frontiers. We see even in biological evolution, for instance, how the development of locomotion permits an organism a much wider range of materials, or how the development of warmblood-edness shields the organism from dependence on the energy level of outside temperature and enables it to function when the outside temperature is unsuitable to the production process. Human history repeats much the same pattern. Thus, the discovery of fire by humans introduced a whole new energy input into human operations and the human economy. Fire not only kept people warm in the winter, which would certainly lead to an increase in the length of life, but also had potential for cooking, which opened up new foods, for pottery which improved food storage among other things, and eventually for metallurgy and the utilization of a whole new range of materials and human artifacts. Fire indeed perhaps was the first great niche creator in the field of human artifacts, though it often took a long time to fill these niches.

How Filling Niches Creates New Ones

Agriculture and the domestication of livestock represented a more efficient use of solar energy on the part of the human race. With agriculture, the solar energy involved in the creation of plants from seed was channeled into food plants and hence increased the food production per acre very substantially. With some of this food draft animals were fed, whose muscles were stronger than those of the human race and therefore represented more efficient solar energy machines than the human body. They also incidentally added to the materials input through their manure, which further increased the yields from agriculture, and perhaps more importantly, ensured permanency in these yields. With draft animals, also, materials could be brought from further away, such as flints, the stones that made Stonehenge and the neolithic villages, and the ores that became metals. After the development of agriculture, everything that happened created new niches. Every time one of these new niches was filled it created further new niches so that we have a constantly expanding and often accelerating rate of change which makes the paleolithic look very stable and stationary indeed.

Role of Exchange and Threat

The relative role of exchange and threat in these processes is a matter of a very interesting, but hard to resolve controversy. The origins of both exchange and of threat are lost in the mists of the past. We can speculate that with the human race divided into small bands ranging over wide areas, threat would precede exchange. The band occupying a favorable situation might be chased out of it by some more aggressive and better organized band. If the conquered are exterminated the threat system certainly comes to an end. If they are reduced to some kind of status like slavery, and provide inputs of muscular energy and perhaps a little know-how and skill for the conquerors, the threat-submission system continues. How old is slavery we certainly do not know.

As soon as we get human beings who are capable of communicating and understanding each other, and live in somewhat different environments so that their products are different, a niche develops for exchange, the outcome of which is profitable to both parties. Thus, we may have one band on the seashore catching fish and another in the forest getting meat. There is then a potential niche for the institution of trade or even of traders. There are old stories, and even some modern examples, of what is called "silent trade," where two groups are so hostile they dare not even meet, but where they have some kind of sacred spot in common. One group spreads, let us say, the fish and then leaves. The other group comes and takes the fish and spreads out meat and also goes away. The first group now comes back and takes the meat, so that exchange is consummated without the groups ever having seen each other. The potential for variety of cultures, however, is so great that there must have been many occasions even in the paleolithic when two relatively unaggressive and nonviolent cultures came together and engaged in trade quite happily.

Specialization Through Threat

The first cities of civilization always seem to depend on the development of an organized threat system which would extract the surplus food from the food producer without giving very much, at least that is tangible, in return. Under these circumstances the relative role of threats and exchange is a tricky question. Sir John Hicks suggests that specialization and the division of labor, which is a great source of increase in productivity, may have originated in the courts of the early rulers, whether priests or kings, who were able to collect enough food, by threat, from the surrounding food producers and with this food feed specialized builders, carpenters, sculptors, metallurgists, potters, weavers, and so on to provide the provisions and artifacts for the temples and palaces of the early cities. Exchange then begins with gifts from one ruler to another which are reciprocated. The ambassador then turns by degrees into a trader and merchant, as the reciprocal exchange of gifts becomes formalized into contractual exchange and trade. There is certainly some historical evidence for this view.

Specialization Through Exchange

Adam Smith, on the other hand, in his famous Chapter Three of *The Wealth of Nations*, points to another mechanism. Trade itself, in evolutionary language, opens up new niches for specialization and specialized production and specialized production increases productivity and opens up new niches for trade and for traders. We thus have a kind of positive feedback process with trade continually creating opportunities to increase production and increased production continually creating opportunities for more trade. Thus, the "division of labor depends on the extent of the market" and the extent of the market also depends on the division of labor. This process is accelerated when the division of labor gets to the point where creation of markets itself becomes specialized through the development of a trading and merchant group specializing in this activity.

Trade Preceded Cities

Actual historical sequences may have been different in different times and places, but it is clear that both these processes have been at work, particularly since the time of the development of the first cities. Even before there were "civilized" cities extensive trade relationships developed, as they did for metals in Europe well before 3000 B.C.; and as we find it, for instance, in the Hopewell Indian culture of Ohio several hundred years ago, where goods came from as much as 1000 or 1500 miles away, to settlements that were no more than villages. One suspects that here again the accidents of cultural development make a lot of difference in particular episodes. The development of culture itself may be something of a "watershed system." At a certain point in its development fairly random events may lead a culture toward peaceful trade, or on the other side of the watershed to aggression, conquest, and threat.

Classical Civilization: The Rise of Technology

What might be called the age of "classical" civilization stretches from ancient Egypt and Sumeria, 3000 B.C., almost to the middle of the nineteenth century. In this period civilization—that is, cities based essentially on a surplus of food from agriculture extracted from the agriculturalists by an organized threat system—spreads geographically around the world both east and west from its origins in West Asia—to Europe, China, Japan, India. It originated perhaps independently in Mesoamerica, but then was overwhelmed by a conquest from Europe in the sixteenth century. There is a long, slow technological improvement in this whole period, with some periods of stagnation, like the Roman Empire from Augustus to Constantine. In the Old World, much of this improvement originated in China and spread across Asia to Europe over about a 300 year interval—the stirrup, the horse collar, the compass, silk cultivation, and perhaps even printing—which all seem to have spread from China, though the origins of all innovations tend to be somewhat obscure.

There is a good deal of evidence that Europe began a long, slow, steady technological improvement shortly after the Fall of Rome, beginning perhaps in the Christian monasteries of the sixth century. The basic evolutionary principle that filling an empty niche creates new niches is seen all the time. Thus, there clearly was an empty niche for the Christian Church in Europe in the late Roman Empire, with the collapse of the older religions and the sense of revelation created by the events of the Gospels. With the fall of the western Roman Empire and the centuries of political disorder and confusion which followed, there was clearly a niche for monasteries and nunneries, where people of moral, intellectual, and spiritual bent could retreat from a disorderly world. Christianity, however, unlike most Eastern religions, believed in the reality of the material world and the sacredness and legitimacy of common labor. "Laborare est orare"—to work is to pray—was the principle of the Benedictines. The fact that Jesus was a carpenter while Buddha was a prince produced what the biologists call a "founder effect" in the evolution of Christian versus Buddhist societies. In the Christian monasteries there were men of intellect who did not despise working with their hands. It is not surprising that the monasteries produced important technological innovations, like the beveled gear and the water wheel, which increased the energy input of economic life.

Interaction of Technology and Social Institutions

Just as the social institutions created niches for new technologies, new technologies created niches for new social institutions. In Europe the ironclad plow which opened up the difficult northern soils, the three-field system, and the horse collar, which tremendously improved the productivity of horses in pulling, increased agricultural productivity after about 800 A.D., and opened up niches for towns. The stirrup and improved metallurgy for the making of swords helped to create knighthood and chivalry. The diminution in central authority as a result of the fall of the Roman Empire, the causes of which are not wholly clear, opened up a large niche for what has been called the "feudal system," with sharp class distinctions between land-owning aristocracy and the peasants or serfs who worked the land, with weak central authority and rather small cities, and a church organization with very widespread spiritual power and occasional temporal power.

The slow, but fairly steady rise in affluence as a result of improved technologies changed the niches for social institutions, and permitted the rise, for instance, of trading cities, such as those of the Hanseatic

League in the early Middle Ages, which increasingly bought their food from the farmer, or from the landlord who collected it from the farmer, and relied on exchange rather than on threat as a means of social organization. Manufacturing of pottery, textiles, implements, art works, and so on, developed in the cities and gave them something to trade with. The Black Death of the mid-fourteenth century, by sharply reducing the population, created new niches and expanded productivity, which perhaps set off the irreversible process that led to science and the modern world.

The 1492 Watershed

We have a feeling of passing some kind of watershed after 1492, with the discovery of America and the trade routes around Africa to Asia. Europe, from being an obscure peninsula at the edge of the civilized world of China and Islam, shifts to being the world center as the improvement in ocean transportation permits the expansion both of trade and of military threat from Europe to coastlines all around the world, and in those continents like the Americas, where resistance was low, to conquests of the interior. At the same time we see the beginnings of science in Copernicus. We also have the Lutheran and the Calvinist Reformations, which can be thought of as increasing the economic productivity of religion, and thereby releasing resources from it— dissolving the monasteries, eliminating expensive pilgrimages, and legitimating work and economic productivity in the world. The niche for Luther, and later for Calvin, was unquestionably partly created by rising affluence, which the Catholic Church perhaps had exploited too vigorously in the building of St. Peter's at Rome. It also represented a rise of more independent centers of power, both economic, political, and spiritual.

Centralization and Decentralization

There seems to be a level of affluence, paradoxically, above which centralized power tends to break up into decentralized units, simply because the centralized power cannot absorb into itself the rising affluence, and there is more possibility of developing new independent centers of power at a distance from the old center. There are certain parallels here in biological evolution, in the very complex problem of the geographical spread of species through the development of greater mobility of the organism (fins, legs, wings) and the impact of this on the structure of local ecosystems.

Evolution of Feudalism into Capitalism

The transformation from feudalism into capitalism in Europe is a classic example of evolutionary transformation. It is impossible to say when one ended and the other began. These were not two clearly identifiable systems in dialectical conflict at any time. The transformation took place imperceptibly by a long series of small changes and mutations, both in technology and in behavioral and organizational structures. We can perhaps distinguish two outstanding processes—one on the side of behavior, and the other in technology. Adam Smith observes (*The Wealth of Nations*, Book 3, Chapter 4) how slowing rising affluence led to increased consumption on the part of the aristocracy, particularly on behalf of their wives, who developed tastes for sumptuousness which previously had been unobtainable. Conspicuous consumption in dress, buildings, houses, carriages, servants, and so on, led to an increased proportion of the income of the aristocracy going into consumption and less into military force, whereas in the earlier period they used the food which they extracted from the peasants and serfs to feed soldiers. Now they had to feed footmen, hairdressers, jewelers, dressmakers, builders, and furniture makers.

Only the centralized authority of the king was able to sustain large military forces. The king's political power rose as that of the barons declined. The technical change which accelerated this process was the development of gunpowder, cannons, and firearms in the sixteenth century. This increased the range of the deadly missile and made medieval castles incapable of providing defense. One sees this dramatically in the Loire Valley; the progression from the great medieval castle of Chinon to Francoise's Chateau of Chambord, which looks like a castle but is not—it could be broken into with a burglar's jimmy—to the completely undefended manor houses of the eighteenth century.

The Gold Inflation of the Sixteenth Century

Another element in this evolutionary transformation of Europe, without parallel in biological systems, was inflation as a result of the discovery of America, the theft of the gold hordes of the Incas and Aztecs by the Spaniards, and the discovery of new gold and silver mines, which led to a very large increase in the gold stock of Europe and about a six-fold inflation through the sixteenth to the early seventeenth century, beginning in Spain but spreading to other European countries. This redistributed income sharply from the old aristocracy to the rising merchant and manufacturing class in the cities. The old feudal rents which originally were based in kind or in labor had by this time largely been commuted to money payments that were hard to change, and the inflation diminished their value and therefore the real income of the landlords, and transferred this to the profits of the entrepreneurial and merchant class.

Why Did Science Develop in Europe? The "Supporting Species" Thesis

One of the really important, but very puzzling questions is what opened up the niche for science in Europe, whereas it did not seem to open up in China, in the Islamic world or in India? The fact that science developed in Europe and not elsewhere gave Europe an enormous advantage in the next 500 years, as the exponential increase in "know-what" as a result of science led to a similar increase in "know-how." This led to the development of new sources of energy and materials and an almost continual expansion of production. The biogenetic potential for science in the human brain had existed as long as the human race. In that sense there was always an empty niche for science. We have here again a "threshold" or "nucleation" problem—that a species has to get to a certain size before it can expand into its niche. In this early period of insecurity and instability a species to survive must in some sense cooperate with other species which have established niches. These offer as it were a protected subniche to the first species in which it can grow to the point at which it can be independent.

In the case of science, these supporting species were, paradoxically enough, the church, which supported Copernicus, even though in some sense science and the church were competitors, and the great diversity of states and even of landlords, which developed as it were isolated niches for individual scientists, like Tycho Brahe. Even universities played a role in this, as in the case of Newton, though on the whole they were not too friendly to the new ideas. In Europe it is clear that this variety of supportive structures was sufficient to permit science to develop to the point where it could be an independent species. This did not really happen until the nineteenth century.

The Special Role of Agriculture

Another principle of particular importance in economic history is that the size of new niches which are opened up by the mutations which occupy an old empty niche is different for different social species. Improvement in the cutting of diamonds will have some impact on the diamond industry, but very little impact on the economy as a whole. An improvement in agriculture will have an enormous impact, both because of the size of the agricultural industry and also because of the resources which it releases for other things. It is roughly true that the division of human activity, especially economic activity, between agriculture and nonagriculture, is a direct function of the productivity of agriculture. A rise in agricultural productivity does change the composition and cost of the food supply, as it moves, for instance, from cereals and vegetables into meat. But this is a relatively small effect compared with the overall limitation of the capacity of the human stomach. If we take the simplest model in which the character of the food supply does not change, then the proportion of the population engaged in food production depends directly on how many people food producers can feed. If it takes three food producing families to produce enough food for four families, then we will have 75 percent of the population in food production and only 25 percent producing other things. If a food producing family can produce food for 20 families—as is roughly the case today in developed countries—5 percent of the population produces all the food it needs and 95 percent of the population will be engaged in nonagricultural production.

The Impact of the Turnip in the Eighteenth Century

An increase in agricultural productivity, therefore, opens up an enormous number of new niches for nonagricultural products. This is a very important principle interpreting what happened in Europe and indeed the whole temperate zone after about 1700. This date marks the beginning of a spectacular and rather steady increase in agricultural productivity, especially in the Netherlands and in England, with the introduction of the turnip, clover, and the four-course rotation. The turnip and other roots produced a crop in what had previously been the fallow fields, fallow in order to get the weeds out. With "horse hoeing husbandry" and root crops, the weeds could be gotten out and a crop produced at the same time. The turnip opened up a large niche for the improvement of livestock. It was now possible to feed livestock through the winter instead of having the great slaughter at Christmas, which was characteristic of the earlier period. This increased protein supplies, which were a major factor in diminishing infant mortality, and in turn created a great population explosion, first in England and then in other parts of Europe, an explosion which led to substantial migration and settlements in North America, Australia, and New Zealand, and so on by English-speaking people.

The "Industrial Revolution" of the Eighteenth Century

The food surplus from agriculture, coupled with the population expansion, opened up a large niche for the development of industry. The so-called "industrial revolution" of the eighteenth century represented a preliminary expansion into this niche in the new industrial towns. The technology, however, was not very far removed from medieval technology, with the exception perhaps of the steam engine, beginning in the early eighteenth century. The eighteenth century in England saw a persistent rise in the use of fossil fuel, particularly coal, which began an enormous expansion of the energy input into the economic system. The discovery of how to smelt iron from coal by Abram Darby of Coalbrookdale in England, began the opening up of a very large niche in metallurgy using fossil fuels instead of wood. This opened up a further niche for machines and eventually for steel-frame buildings, bridges, railroads, and so on, which would never have come into being if the iron and steel industry had to rely on wood as a source of energy, except perhaps in the United States, where at that time wood was still plentiful.

Science-based Technology After 1850

Somewhere between 1850 and 1860 we find economic development going into a new gear, substantially accelerated by the rise of science-based technology and industry. Up to this time the contribution of science to technology had been rather meager. The steam engine (1711) owed nothing to thermodynamics (about 1818). Thermodynamics owed a good deal to the steam engine. The technological changes of the eighteenth-century industrial revolution almost all came out of what might be called "folk technology" and they owed very little to the rising body of science. There were improvements in cartography and perhaps some mechanical devices which could be attributed to science, but these were fairly small.

From 1850 on, however, we observe a great change, beginning perhaps with the chemical industry in the 1860's with the development of analine dyes, which would have been inconceivable without Dalton, Kekulé, and Mendeleef. This industry expanded explosively until today we have produced tens of thousands of chemical substances unknown to the world before. There is, incidentally, a great danger in this as well as promise, for we are already producing innumerable substances which the biosphere has never had to deal with before, some of which might have catastrophic effects on it.

In the next generation comes the electrical industry; the first power station in 1888 opened up an enormous number of new niches. It transformed the home and the household, with electric lights, electric appliances, enormously diminishing the niche for domestic servants. It transformed the manufacturing industry. In spite of the fact that well over half the original energy input is lost in the transmission of electricity, it is so subdividable and convenient that the overall energy input per dollar of real GNP fell sharply in the first half of the twentieth century in the developed societies. Electric power led to the phonograph, radio, television, which in turn led to enormous social change. It led also to computers, the ultimate consequences of which are still very far from clear.

The Impact of Oil and Gas

Another profound source of evolutionary change was the discovery of oil and then natural gas, beginning in Titusville, Pennsylvania, in 1859. This developed an extremely cheap and convenient source of storable energy for the economic system. The sequence here may have begun first with the development of the whaling industry as a result of improvements in shipping and whaling techniques in the early-nineteenth century. This led to the expansion and production of whale oil, mainly for household illumination. As the whales began to be overkilled, whaling diminished, which left an empty niche for household illumination, which was filled by kerosene, the first important commercial product of oil. The production of kerosene, however, produced gasoline as a byproduct, unwanted in the first instance but which then opened up a niche for the automobile, which was rapidly filled. This led to profound changes in the structure of cities, changing from an essentially wheel structure with a "hub" and radial lines of railroads going out from it, to a "chicken wire" structure, with decaying centers, expanding suburbs, and rings of shopping centers and industrial plants. It is not an exaggeration to say that the change in economic life and output in my grandfather's life, say about 1860 to 1930, was the most spectacular period of technical and economic change in the whole history of the human race. It was strictly an evolutionary, not a revolutionary, change. It happened because new niches were continually opened up for products, techniques, and new forms of organization. The rate of mutation was very high, so that these niches were rapidly filled. Every niche that was filled opened up new niches elsewhere and produced an explosive process of expansion!

The Organizational Revolution

The development of new technologies and commodities likewise produced large changes in organizational and social structure, which in turn reacted on the new technologies. Around about 1870 there begins what I have called the "organizational revolution," a large increase in the optimum size of organizations of all kinds—corporations, labor unions, national states, churches, and so on. This is partly the result of the development of new commodities and technologies, like electricity and the telephone, the telegraph and the typewriter. This tremendously increased the capacity of upper members of a hierarchy to communicate with the lower members over increasingly wide geographical areas. In the days when communication had to go by pony express, and even in the same building by little notes carried around by office boys, the capacity for the "boss" to communicate with the people at the edge of the organization, and for them to communicate with the boss, was very limited. This severely limited the size of organizations, and the optimum scale was fairly small, beyond which diseconomies of scale would set in very sharply. In 1860 the largest organizations of the world—governments, churches, businesses—rarely employed more than a few thousand people. The Catholic Church looks like an exception to this rule, but that was because the amount of communication required between the Vatican and the parish priests was very small.

After 1870 organizations began to grow very rapidly, until today we have giants like General Motors, Exxon, the United States Department of Defense, the Soviet Union, all of which would have been inconceivable without the telephone, the typewriter, and, later, the computer. We see a similar phenomenon on a much smaller scale even in agriculture, where the economies of scale are very meager but where the size, even of the family farm, has increased more than tenfold in the last 100 years as a result of telephones, tractors, eleborate farm machinery, agricultural colleges, and county agents.

The Impact on War and the International System

A science-based technology has also had a very profound effect on the nature of the international system and on war. The development of long-range missiles with nuclear warheads has created a change in the system just as profound as the invention of gunpowder. The national state is now as inherently defenseless as was the feudal castle. Whether we can realize this before we destroy ourselves through a system of unilateral national defense is perhaps the most critical question in the future. This is a situation where unless there is rapid evolutionary change in the images, institutions, and technology of defense, we are likely to have revolutionary change in nuclear war, the consequences of which are completely unpredictable.

The Slowdown in the Rate of Change

No growth process is exponential for very long. All of them follow what are called logistic curves with eventually diminishing rates of growth. The great expansion of science-based technology since 1850 is no exception to this rule. The rate of change was far greater in my grandfather's life than it has been in mine. Short of revolutionary change, my grandchildren may see less change than I have. I grew up as a boy in the

1920s essentially in the "modern world," with telephones, skyscrapers, automobiles, airplanes, radio, movies, electricity, and so on. My grandfather, growing up in the 1860s, grew up in a world of horses, very primitive machines, candles, an occasional steam engine and steam train, but on the whole a world which was not enormously different technologically from his grandfather's or his grandfather's grandfather. I have seen more quantitative changes than qualitative; more automobiles, faster airplanes, brighter lights, but almost the only qualitative changes I have seen in ordinary daily life are television, throughways, and perhaps the computer and the jet plane across the oceans. Even nuclear energy has made extremely little impact on daily life.

Evolution and Revolution

When we look at the development of economic institutions and organizations on a world scale we see both evolutionary and revolutionary change in the twentieth century. The evolutionary change is quite large. We see the rise of the giant corporation especially the multinational corporation; the development of the welfare state with social security, public health and the like; a great rise in the educational system beyond elementary levels, and a substantial increase in governmental regulation. We also see striking evolutionary changes in fashion, architecture, dress, sex and family life, and so on.

Nevertheless, there have also been revolutionary changes in the development of centrally planned economies and communist states. Technology, the occupational structure, and the commodity production of these states has followed evolutionary lines and is not very different from that of the capitalist states, though perhaps with greater inefficiency. The social institutions, however, are markedly different. Capital markets have become illegal, and private economic organizations have been reduced to a relatively small part of the economy, though without the farmers' private plots the socialist countries might well have collapsed from the sheer inefficiency of collectivized agriculture. The bulk of the economy of these countries, however, is organized by state-owned organizations, coordinated by a central plan rather than through the relative price structure and the operations of the market. This is a very profound change which is most unlikely to happen in an evolutionary manner.

War Breeds Revolution

Significantly, with the possible exception of Cuba, communist revolution came about as a result of war and indeed of unusually catastrophic war, which is perhaps the main revolutionary element in the existing system. War created a niche for communist governments simply due to the collapse of the governments which preceded them. This has profoundly changed the evolutionary structure of the system, though not as much perhaps as might appear at first sight. The communist countries have not produced much in the way of new technology and have mostly copied their technology from the capitalistic countries, with some possible exceptions like the space enterprise. Politically the communist societies rest on a highly tyrannical, centralized threat system as in Russia, or a centralized monopoly of communication and persuasion as in China. Whether these systems can survive increasing affluence and the questioning and decentralization that this is almost certain to produce is one of the interesting questions of the next hundred years.

Two potentially revolutionary changes still threaten capitalist societies. The major one is nuclear war, from which it is extremely unlikely that they will recover unchanged and which will so completely discredit any existing order that the nearest available revolutionary transformation will undoubtedly be sought. Another more remote possibility is an internal economic collapse of capitalism on the lines of the Great Depression of 1929-1932. There are government policies that could produce this, particularly if we are not prepared to offset a sharp decline in Gross Private Domestic Investment and in profit, or if our financial and fiscal policies put the choice before us of hyperinflation or unemployment. Much greater certainty attaches to the exhaustion of cheap energy and materials, which we will explore in the next chapter. This takes us, however, beyond history into the future.

Note

1. The "mesolithic"—a period of harsher environments due to the end of the ice age, in many places possibly resulting in a deterioration in human welfare, is often inserted between the paleolithic and the neolithic.

CHAPTER 5

The Economics of Energy and Entropy in Evolutionary Perspective

Thermodynamics as a Post-Newtonian Paradigm

The fact that economics was a well-developed discipline long before the rise of thermodynamics may account for its lingering Newtonian flavor and for current attacks on it in the name of thermodynamics. We certainly cannot blame Adam Smith, writing in the 1770s, for not being aware of thermodynamics, which begins with Carnot, about 1817, did not even really identify its fundamental concepts of entropy until Clausius in 1865, and developed its basic theoretical structure with Boltzman in the 1870s. The great advocate of the thermodynamic approach to economics is Nicholas Georgescu-Roegen, whose work on *The Entropy Law and the Economic Process*[1] was a landmark. The economics profession, it is true, has not paid much attention to it, but there is now developing almost a cult of entropy which takes its cue from this work.[2] The first entropy economist indeed might well be William S. Jevons, ironically enough one of the founders of the marginal utility school, which helped to make economics even more Newtonian than it was before. However, in his book, *The Coal Question*,[3] in 1865, Jevons clearly anticipates most of the concerns of entropy economics, particularly in regard to exhaustible resources and to the importance of energy throughput to the system.

There are two great principles of thermodynamics. The first law is the law of conservation—that energy can be transformed into various forms but cannot either be created or destroyed in a closed system. The famous second law of thermodynamics can be stated in a good many ways. Originally, like much of thermodynamics, it comes out of the theory of the steam engine. The steam engine, indeed, which was developed around 1711, predates not only thermodynamics, but even economics. As someone has said, thermodynamics owed a great deal to the steam engine; the steam engine owed very little to thermodynamics. It was Carnot who really developed the theory of the steam engine and the principle that for energy to be applied to doing work—that is, the movement of matter through space—there must be temperature differences between parts of the machine, and the act of performing the work reduces these temperature differences, so that the energy, while it remains constant, becomes less available. The concept of the unavailability of energy for doing work was formalized by Clausius into the concept of entropy. As this was defined as unavailability, it means that there is a constant increase in entropy in any closed system.

Entropy as Negative Potential

I have argued that the entropy concept was in fact rather unfortunate, in the sense that it was a negative concept, almost like phlogiston, which turned out to be negative oxygen. The positive, general concept which corresponds to negative entropy is that of potential and this concept has very broad implications far beyond the narrow confines of thermodynamics. We could then restate the second law in a generalized form by saying that if anything happens it is because there is a potential for it happening, and after it has happened, that part of the potential has been used up. We thus translate the entropy law into the law of diminishing potential, which certainly seems much more intuitively comprehensible than a law of increasing entropy. In thermodynamics, therefore, we could say that if energy makes anything happen, it is because there was a thermodynamic potential for it happening in the form of a temperature difference, and that once it has happened, that potential has been used up, so that the energy has less potential than before.

Stating the second law in terms of the using up of potential opens up the possibility that potential may be recreated. In thermodynamics the creation of thermodynamic potential has not actually been observed. However, it must have been created in the first place unless we suppose that the universe started infinite time ago with zero entropy and infinite thermodynamic potential, which is a pretty wild idea. If thermodynamic potential was created once, of course, it might be created again. We really do not understand this process.

In open systems, like the earth, thermodynamic potential is recreated all the time, particularly by the throughput of energy from the sun. The second law in effect says that water runs downhill because its potential energy is higher at the top than it is at the bottom. Once it has gotten to the bottom, however, that potential is used up. If the earth were a closed system, all the water would soon run downhill into the sea and that would be the end of rivers and certainly the end of waterwheels. The potential energy of water, however, is continually reestablished by the evaporation of water from the oceans by the sun and its precipitation on the land as rain or snow, so that waterwheels, at any rate, theoretically can go on as long as the sun does.

In biological systems, likewise, we see the constant exhaustion of old potential and the recreation of new. Every fertilized egg contains the potential for the organism that it can produce. If the environment is favorable in terms of energy and materials, the genetic information in the egg reorganizes the world around it and produces the organism. As the process proceeds, however, this potential is gradually exhausted until the organism finally ages and dies. This is an example of the generalized second law. In the interval, however, new eggs are likely to have been fertilized and biological potential recreated. An individual organism, therefore, follows the inexorable law of exhaustion of potential. A whole population of similar individuals, however, can go on for a very long time, at least until its evolutionary potential is exhausted, whatever that is, provided, of course, that the earth remains an open system and that there is a continual throughput of energy from the sun.

Entropy and Evolution

The relation of energy and entropy to the evolutionary process should now be clear. Biological evolution can only take place in open systems like the earth, in which there is a throughput of energy. This is because even though biological and indeed societal evolution also are essentially processes in genetic information and know-how, this information cannot be coded or transmitted unless the know-how of the genetic structure can result in a growth process that produces the organism. This growth process requires a throughput of energy. The organism that results then has a capacity for recreating the biological potential involved in the genetic structure, through, for instance, fertilizing a new egg. This principle does not of course violate the second law of thermodynamics; entropy is increasing in the sun as its potential is being used up and of course it will eventually burn out in some billions of years. And unless the evolutionary potential is recreated by migrating to other parts of the universe, as it may well have done by that time, the evolution that began on earth will come to an end.

Production, as we have seen, is a process of how the genotype creates the phenotype, as the fertilized egg creates its organism. This involves a suitable environment in terms of energy, materials, space, and time. These are the limiting factors of production. These limits may be narrow or broad depending on the nature of the genetic information and the degree to which the process can tolerate a wide or a narrow range of environments in the limiting factors. Such tolerance is likely to produce evolutionary success, but there seem to be limits to it. What determines the limits to tolerance is not, I think, well understood. It rather looks as if tolerance has to be paid for in terms of smaller niches for tolerant species in particular systems than are obtained by those species that are intolerant, but specialized to the systems.

This problem relates also to the impact of catastrophe on evolution. The dinosaurs became extinct and mammals survived because in some sense the mammals were more tolerant of adverse environments, perhaps because of their greater degree of control of body temperature. There must be limits to the extent to which an increase in the complexity of genetic structure can create tolerance, but where these limits are is very hard to say. In the human race, certainly, the capacity to create artifacts has enormously increased the environmental tolerance of the human organism. We have been able to survive at the poles, at the bottom of the sea, and even on the surface of the moon where no other living creature can survive, because of the artifacts with which we surround ourselves in the shape of clothing, submarines, and space suits. The capacity for tolerance of environmental change, which is implicit in the development of consciousness and intelligence, is a very important element in our expectations of the future, especially those of the long run.

As Schrodinger[4] has said, "Evolution is the segregation of entropy." That is, it involves the creation of these extraordinary little islands of order in the cells, the plants, the animals, the human race and its artifacts, at the cost indeed of disorder elsewhere, the elsewhere here being mainly in the sun, although it may also be in other parts of the earth. Another way of saying the same thing is that "evolution is pollution." The same concept of the creation of order in one place always involves a greater disorder elsewhere. The important thing is that the elsewhere should be really elsewhere and that the segregation of entropy be maintained.

Entropy in Social and Economic Systems

How, then, does all this apply to social and economic systems? We see the same two processes continually at work here as we see in the biosphere, the continuous exhaustion of potential and its equally continuous recreation or replenishment. There have been times in the history of the human race when exhaustion may have predominated over replenishment. Even in hunting and gathering societies the environment has been overwhelmed and overgathered, potential has been exhausted, and there may have been corresponding declines in human population and in human welfare. There have been other times when replenishment has far outweighed exhaustion and the niche of the human race has expanded and its welfare increased. There is some indication, also, that in those periods when exhaustion has predominated and the niche of the human race has shrunk and its welfare diminished, this very fact has often stimulated the development of new technologies, the discovery of new resources, and a new outburst of replenishment. Thus, the development of agriculture may well have been the result of a period of increasing exhaustion of hunting and gathering resources, of where indeed necessity was the mother of invention. Another example of this may be the discovery of the utilization of coal for the smelting of iron and steel and other metals, following an increasing exhaustion of wood in Western Europe. It is curious that only a few years before the publication of Jevons's book on the coal question (in which he foresaw the exhaustion of coal) oil and natural gas were discovered, to the enormous replenishment of known exhaustible resources. Even this may have been stimulated by the exhaustion of whale oil!

The Significance of Limiting Factors

When we try to explain the composition of any ecological system, whether of biological or of human artifacts, the position and the dominance of the limiting factors is the thing that on the whole we have to look for, at least if we hold the genetic factor of know-how constant. It is the most limiting of the limiting factors that is significant, and this, of course, can change quite suddenly. In the Arctic tundra, for instance, the low throughput of solar energy is undoubtedly the main limiting factor, for only those species can survive that can tolerate it. In the desert, the limiting factor is water; in some cases it is soils; in some cases it may even be wind. In some cases it may be a particular material, like salt, of which there may be too much or too little, or even some trace element. It is not surprising that the variety of ecosystems is enormous and that the intellectual task of understanding them is very large and difficult.

In understanding the dynamics of social systems also, the search for limiting factors is very important. Sometimes indeed the limiting factor is energy and materials, as in the case of what might be called the "harsh cultures" of the Eskimo, or the Bushmen of Africa, where agriculture is clearly impossible and building materials are scarce. The basic limiting factor may be energy in the case of the Eskimo; water in the case of the Bushmen. In many cases, however, the limiting factor is essentially genetic. Thus, the failure of societies to develop may be due to failure of the human learning process, especially perhaps a failure of the moral learning process in the society, which produces values and attitudes that are inimical to invention and to risk taking, or to productive capital accumulation. The institutions of a society may be very important limiting factors here, insofar as they either encourage or prevent people who are capable of social mutation, or who are imaginative and creative, from occupying positions of power in which their creativity can be expressed. The institutions which determine the allocation of power in society, indeed, are extremely important in determining its development. If those who have the power lack the will, and those who have the will lack the power, development will not take place.

Efficiency Concepts Always Imply Human Valuations

In applying physical concepts like energy and entropy to social and economic systems, certain pitfalls have to be avoided, some of which indeed are very easy to fall into. In the first place, it is very important to recognize that all significant efficiency concepts rest on human valuations and that efficiency concepts which are based on purely physical inputs and outputs may not be significant in human terms, or at least their significance has to be evaluated. All efficiency concepts involve a ratio of output to input in a process. The more output per unit of input, the more efficient we suppose it to be. The significance of the efficiency concept, however, depends on the significance of the outputs and inputs in terms of human valuations.

Thus, simple energy efficiency always has to be interpreted very carefully. In strict terms, of course, because of the law of conservation, the total energy output of any process must be equal to the total input, and all energy efficiencies are equal to 1.0. When we speak of energy efficiency, however, we are always referring to some proportion of the output which we regard in some sense as significant. Thus, the energy efficiency of an electric power station is the ratio of its output of electricity energy to its input of fuels and other sources, which should include presumably the energy loss involved in the depreciation of the capital that would be required to replace it. If, however, the energy output is in a form which is more highly valued in terms of human values than the energy input, a process can be quite energy inefficient and still very efficient in terms of human values. Electric power production is a good example of this. In terms of energy, it is very inefficient. It is striking, however, that the rise of the electric power industry, particularly between about 1910 and 1950, coincided with a sharp increase in the total energy efficiency of the economy as measured by the real GNP per unit of energy input.[5]

Similarly, the so-called "second law efficiency," which roughly means the amount of increase in entropy per unit of energy input, may have very little significance indeed in human valuation terms, depending on whether the system is one in which the restoration of the potential of the system is easy and cheap or difficult and expensive, and this in turn depends to a very large extent on the presence or absence of substitutes for the various inputs. The net energy concept, also, developed particularly by Howard and Elisabeth Odum,[6] is of some interest in itself, but it should never be used as a surrogate for human valuations.

Dangers of the Entropy Concept

It is very dangerous also to apply the entropy concept in an absolute form, as Rifkin tends to do, [7] for it will almost lead to the conclusion that evolution was impossible! As it happened, it must be possible. Whether entropy is an ultimate law of the universe we really do not know. We know virtually nothing about the potential of the universe for recreating thermodynamic potential, or for that matter, in a more general form, evolutionary potential. The great poetic vision of Teilhard de Chardin, of the creation of all subsequent evolutionary potential in the big bang, which potential is realized increasingly until a new universe is created, is at least as plausible as that of the entropy religion, which postulates a wholly inexplicable state of low entropy and high potential at the beginning, which potential is never recreated but constantly eroded, until the universe ends not with a bang but a whimper in the "heat death" at which everything is at the same temperature and nothing more can happen.

Economic Applications: Time as a Resource Inheritance

Looking now more closely at the economic applications of these principles, we find we have to take account much more explicitly than we have hitherto done of the time resource. An exhaustible resource has to be allocated through time. This is a problem that is not solved by simply pointing out that the resource is exhaustible. This involves human valuations over time and there are many philosophies about this. Should we "Take therefore no thought for the morrow: for the morrow shall take thought for the things of itself,"[8] which is the advice of a very well regarded authority? Should we "eat, drink, and be merry, for tomorrow we die" to use a somewhat less well-regarded adage? Or should we husband every drop and grain, and use as little in the present as we possibly can, and spare all that we can for the future?

The question "What has posterity ever done for me?" attributed to Marx (Groucho), is at least not a silly question. My own view indeed is that it has an answer, which is that posterity enables us to pay the debt that we cannot repay to our ancestors. We are all inheritors of countries, cities, libraries, universities, a great body of human knowledge, buildings, literature and art, all of which we did nothing to produce, and there is something in human nature which makes us uncomfortable about getting things for nothing. Our terms of trade can be too good for moral as well as too bad for physical comfort. We have always been suspicious of fortune's smiles, suspecting that they are all too often a prelude to frowns. To receive a gift produces what the Japanese call "on," a sense of guilt and uneasiness which lasts until a return gift is made. Receiving gifts lowers our status, often in our own eyes; giving them increases it. So the gifts we have received from the past create a sense of obligation which can only be relieved by gifts to the future. This is presumably why people plan to die with a net worth, which they pass on to someone else, whereas a purely selfish, self-contained economic man would so plan his estate that he would leave nothing. A *New Yorker* cartoon once showed the lawyer reading the will to a depressed group of relatives, which read, "Being of good health and of sound mind, I blew it all!"

To leave an inheritance, however, we must have a sense of community with those who will live in the future. The strongest sense of community historically has been in the family, which is no doubt why in almost all societies the estates of those who die *intestate*, without wills, pass to the nearest relations. When family obligations are reasonably satisfied, people leave estates to good causes, sometimes even to their governments. It is very rare, however, to leave estates to the unborn, with whom it is hard to have a sense of community because we do not know who they are. In the case of exhaustible resources, however, it may be precisely the unborn who are significant, who will benefit or suffer from our decisions. As they have no votes, however, except through their power to raise the sympathy of the living, they are likely to be highly underrepresented in the decision-making process.

The Economic Theory of Exhaustible Resources

Curiously enough, economics does come up with something of an answer to the problem of the rate of use of exhaustible resources. This depends on the fact that virtually every economic society of any substantial complexity will have something like a rate of return on capital. This is likely to be a range of numbers depending on risks, liquidity, and other elements, ranging from a low real rate of interest on extremely safe, short-run, and liquid securities, to high rates of return on high-risk and illiquid investments. The distinction between rates of interest on loans, bonds, and contractual securities and rates of profit on processes of production which involve real capital is important for many purposes but can be neglected in this case because, for any particular situation we cannot suppose that the financial markets throw up a rate of return which is appropriate to each case, through buying and selling of notes, bonds, stocks, and so on. There will then be some average rate of return, representing a rate of growth of the net value of capital, or net worth. This rate of growth is a reflection of what might be called the human valuation of the efficiency of the use of time.

Efficiency, in terms of human valuations, is not adequately measured by simply the ratio of the value of output to the value of input in a process. The significance of this ratio depends on the time interval between the input and the output. Suppose, for instance, that we had a process in which the input was $1 million and the output $2 million, supposing for the sake of simplicity that input all takes place at one time and the output at another time. The significance of this would depend very much on the time interval. If there is a million dollars' worth of input and two million dollars' worth of output after one year, then the rate of return is 100 percent. If the output only comes back after about 14 years, the rate of return is only 5 percent. Obviously, the two processes are the same ratio of output to input, but usually we prefer the one which took the shorter time, for this in terms of human valuations would be more efficient as measured by the rate of return. "Dollars" here refer to some measure of overall human valuations. This may not correspond to dollars in the accounting sense, as some accounting dollars may be more highly valued than others, depending on who gets them and how they are gotten, though it is not wholly unreasonable to take accounting dollars as at least a first approximation to human valuations.

It is a general economic principle that resources are properly distributed when the real rate of return on the processes involved in them in their use is appropriate to the degree of risk, uncertainty, unpleasantness, illiquidity, and so on of the occupation. These appropriate rates will center around some kind of overall average rate which represents the overall evaluation of the society of the future. If this is high, say 20 percent, this means that future values are discounted very sharply. At 20 percent discount, $100 one year from now is only reckoned to be worth $83.33; $100 100 years from now would now only be worth $0.0000012! If the average rate of return is only 1 percent per annum, $100 a year from now is worth $99.01 now, $100 100 years from now is worth \$36.97; 1000 years from now it is worth half a cent! If the rate of return is zero, then \$100 a year from now or 1000 years from now is worth \$100 now. This, indeed, some moralists have argued, is the way we should reckon. All times should be equally valuable, and posterity should have equal rights with the living. There are very few, if any, societies who ever actually achieve this.

The rate of return on the ownership of an exhaustible resource depends on which of two options is exercised—leaving it unextracted, or extracting it. If its price is expected to rise rapidly enough, relative to its present price, the rate of return on leaving it in the ground can be greater than the rate of return of extracting it; then it should be left in the ground. In the early stage of the exhaustion of a resource, therefore, when it is very plentiful, the price is low and it is not rising, for any rise in price produces new discoveries. Its production on this criterion should then be high. As it becomes exhausted, however, and its reserves decline, its price begins to rise and increasingly it pays to diminish its extraction and leave more of it for the future, which further raises the price. The rise in price increases the return *both* on extracting it *and* on not extracting it—it is not easy to say which will predominate. If the price rises, of course, there is always the possibility that substitutes will be found or that new and quite unfamiliar sources will be discovered, and this might cause the price to fall again.

I am by no means suggesting that this is a final and completely satisfactory solution to the problem. All of the values may not correspond to the societal values, because, for instance, of societal costs which are not counted in the accounting system, like pollution or environmental destruction, because they are not part of the property and exchange system of society. There is also the possibility of ethical critique of a society's preferences in these matters, which, if it is effective, may change the preferences. The critique usually seems to be in the direction of saying that we do not pay enough attention to posterity and that, therefore, the rate of return at which we calculate should be lower. But it could conceivably go the other way and chastize the society for sacrificing the present generation unnecessarily. Indeed, there is some case for this, for the very existence of economic development is in some sense a tax on the present generation for the benefit of the future, and the question can at least be raised as to whether this is just. The question is not only "What has posterity done for me?" but also "What will posterity do to deserve the sacrifices which its ancestors (that is, us) have made?" Socialist societies, oddly enough, have quite a strong tendency to sacrifice the present generation for the supposed benefit of posterity, to the point where the present generation can have some quite legitimate complaints.

The Role of Relative Prices

A common mistake which is made both in thinking about the problem of exhaustible resources and in policies directed toward it is to neglect the very important role of the price system. The relative price structure, by determining the terms of trade of individuals in different occupations and the rate of return on the use of resources in different occupations, has a very important effect not only on the conservation of resources but also on the discovery of new resources. It is a fairly general principle that if something is cheap, we will neither conserve it nor look for substitutes; whereas when something is perceived as expensive, interest in conserving it rises substantially and the search for substitutes is likely to be attractive. It is a sound economic principle, therefore, that because of the time factor in both exhaustion and replenishment, policies should be directed toward anticipating the future price structure in the present. If we have something like water in some parts of the country, or oil and natural gas, which is plentiful and fairly cheap now but which has a high probability of being scarcer and more expensive later on, there is a great deal to be said for making it more expensive now. This can easily be done through the tax system, especially through the combination of a tax on consumption of the finished product, which will raise its price, with perhaps a subsidy on the discovery of new sources and new production. This has to be done carefully to avoid excessive economic rents to old producers, but there is no fundamental reason why this cannot be done. It is astonishing what little attention we pay to this very obvious response to the problem. We preach conservation and then try to make the thing we want to conserve cheap, which will discourage conservation.

Certainly an intelligent use of the price system is not the only way to deal with these problems of exhaustible resources, but it could go a long way. The current energy problem is a good case in point. It seems highly probable that the real price of fossil fuels, especially the more convenient ones like oil and natural gas, will continue to rise in the foreseeable future. Some estimates suggest that the overall real price of fossil fuels might well quadruple in the next fifty years. At present, the American economy devotes something like 7 percent of its GNP to production and imports of energy. As the price rises, this percentage, of course, will increase. As the price increases, however, large conservation efforts will be made. One estimate suggests that we could easily conserve 25 percent of our present energy consumption by the next generation, even without any drastic change in techniques.[9] It seems unlikely, therefore, that energy inputs will rise to more than 15 percent or at most 20 percent of the GNP by the early twenty-first century. This would leave, let us say, 85 percent, or at worst 80 percent, for other things, instead of 93 percent. This is clearly not catastrophic, although certainly on the debit side of the accounts. Relatively small increases in productivity in these other things could easily offset the rise in the real cost of energy. This at least puts the doomsday predictions in some sort of perspective.

Prospect for the Next Century: Energy

This is not to say, of course, that there is nothing to worry about. With a virtual certainty that the earth's population will rise to 8 billion by the early years of the next century, barring a catastrophic nuclear war or epidemics, the pressure on exhaustible resources of all kinds will continue to grow, particularly in the light of a strong urge on the part of the poor countries to get richer and even a certain possibility that the rich countries might get somewhat richer. The biggest immediate energy crisis is wood. Serious deforestation, particularly in the tropics, is coming simply with the growth of population as well as with a certain amount of commercial exploitation. Up to now, this has been offset to some extent by an expansion of forests in the temperate zone and the less thickly populated regions, but this too may be threatened if the rising cost of oil and gas turn people increasingly towards wood as a source of home heating. It is well to remember that the eastern seaboard of the United States was almost completely denuded of wood by the year 1860, partly for buildings and partly for heat, and this could happen again.

Whether the world oil production peaks out in 1990, as is frequently predicted, or if we have a lot of good luck, in 2010, does not make much difference. Cheap oil and natural gas will certainly be gone before the middle of the twenty-first century. Coal will last a little longer. If it becomes a major substitute for oil and gas, it too has an expectancy of not more than 100 or 200 years on a world scale. The existing nuclear industry is no better off than oil and gas. The light water reactor, simply because of the scarcity of uranium 235, does not have a life expectancy of much more than 50 years, even if this is not cut short by political forces, as it may well be. Of known energy stocks technology, only the breeder reactor looks as if it has a horizon of several thousand years. The light water reactor only burns up about 1/200th or a little more of the uranium, but with the breeder reactor we can burn up perhaps 70-80 percent of it, which looks like a potential for electricity for the human race, at any rate, on the order of thousands of years. The breeder, if used on a large scale, still has serious unsolved problems of fuel processing, waste disposal, and of the increased potential for nuclear weapons. However, unless we solve the problem of nuclear weapons very soon, breeder reactors or no breeder reactors, we are likely to have a nuclear war, certainly within a century. There is some doubt as to whether the proliferation of plutonium really adds much in balance to the problem, though perhaps it does. Somewhere over the hill is fusion, still an unsolved problem, and one that might turn out to be soluble, simply because of the extraordinary difficulties of containing and controlling the reaction. Unless we go to the deuterium reaction, and there is no certainty in that, even fusion power, because the present techniques depend on lithium which is a fairly scarce element, does not look any better than the breeder-fission reaction, as a long-range source of energy.

Solar energy, the last ultimate sustainable resource for a continuing social system with high energy throughput, is a complex set of question marks. Up to something like 20 percent of our present energy consumption, it looks fairly good, in terms of improved passive solar heat for houses and conservation of space heating through better insulation, together with passive solar heat for many industrial processes. The technology in large measure is already here; all that is needed is a continued rise in the price of oil and natural gas and these installations will be made, though there is some possibility that we might run into material shortages if it is done on a very large scale. The next most optimistic prospect is the photoelectric cell, tremendous improvements in which have been made in the last few years. If this continues and if electricity storage can be improved, the possibility of each house providing its own electricity from solar cells on the roof is at least not absurd. We may turn out to be grateful for urban sprawl, for this would be impossible with apartment houses and skyscrapers. Other possibilities on the horizon might be direct solar photoelectrolysis of water, producing hydrogen and oxygen; the hydrogen can then be burned and also transported in pipes, which already exist for natural gas. Improved or even artificial photosynthesis opens up some possibilities of growing things to burn, so-called biomass energy, which the human race has done for a very long time, but on a large scale this would be competitive with the food supply and would have to be much more efficient than it is now to be practicable as a substitute for existing sources. Solar satellites in space projecting microwave beams to the earth still remain, perhaps happily, in the realm of science fiction and research proposals. OTEC (Ocean Thermal Exchange Conversion), using the temperature difference between surface and deep water to drive dynamos and produce electricity, has some potential in the next 50 years, but is at the moment no challenge to OPEC!

The great problem with solar energy is that it is very diffuse. The energy that falls on a square yard, if it was utilized 100 percent by turning it into electricity, would hardly be enough to light more than a few lamps. Furthermore, most active solar proposals involve the production of electricity, which is very nice stuff but up to now not much good for driving a car, though pretty fair for driving trains. It would not be a substitute for gasoline. The problem of light, cheap, and capacious electricity storage remains unsolved, even though there have been very large payoffs for this for the public utilities for over 100 years. This suggests that the very problem is extremely difficult, though one can never be sure that it is insoluble. Because collecting solar energy requires a lot of space, it may run into a serious limitation on this account. The economizing of space, for instance, through higher crop yields and skyscrapers, has been an important element in economic development, and an extensive use of solar collectors would reverse this process.

Prospects for Materials

As we look at the somewhat longer perspective, materials shortages may loom even larger than energy. The most critical material for both the biosphere and the sociosphere (the sphere of all human beings and their artifacts) is undoubtedly water. And while a great deal of this is a renewable resource because of rain and snow, in particular regions even this can be an important limiting factor. In some areas like the Western Great Plains in the United States, agriculture is exploiting a water mine of old accumulated water which has a life expectancy perhaps even less than oil. Furthermore, water is used not only as the input of life processes and virtually all industrial processes, it is also used as an output to carry excrement and pollution, the unwanted products of processes of production. In order to do this there must be enough of it, and in many places it is already becoming scarce.

Along with water, the virtual necessity for all processes of production, both biological and human, is air, especially of course the oxygen in it, although nitrogen is also significant for some processes, especially the fixation of nitrogen both biological and human. Nitrogen, incidentally, is a good example of the replenishment process. In the late nineteenth century there was a big scare that natural deposits of nitrogen fertilizer were rapidly being exhausted and that this would have disastrous consequences for developed agriculture, especially of Europe, which had come to depend heavily on Chilean nitrates. It was not long, however, before the Haber process for the fixation of nitrogen from the air was able to tap a virtually inexhaustible supply, although at the cost of course of using fossil fuel.

In some places, especially cities like Los Angeles and Denver, we have to worry about air pollution, for air is also a source of disposal of unwanted products, even though there has also been much improvement in the last few decades, for instance in Pittsburgh and London. Two larger problems, however, have surfaced. The more immediate one is acid rain, which comes from power stations and industrial plants, particularly as they put sulphur or nitrates in one form or another into the air and it produces sulphuric or nitric acid. This has already caused serious concern in many areas downwind of industrial concentrations, such as New England and Sweden, and it does seem to be a moderately intractible problem.

The CO_2 Problem

The other problem which is receiving a good deal of attention is the possible impact of increasing the carbon dioxide content of the atmosphere as a result of the burning of fossil fuels of all kinds, but particularly of coal. Carbon dioxide in itself, even in substantially increased quantities, would seem to be innocuous to human beings and most animals, and positively beneficial to most plants. The worry here is the possible effect on climate. Some meteorological models project a substantial warming of the earth, especially at the poles, with consequent changes in the circulatory systems bringing about large local changes in rainfall, as well as in temperature. Certainly a shift of climate belts northward would have very drastic effects on human settlement. There is also a fear of the melting of the icecaps and perhaps quite a sudden slide of the west Antarctic icecap into the ocean, which could raise the level of the ocean almost immediately by 25 feet, which would have dramatic and drastic effects on the human race, as a considerable proportion of it lives under the 25 feet contour. Certainly the capital reconstruction that would be involved is horrifying to contemplate. Among other things, every port in the world would have to be rebuilt and large parts of the port cities. A considerable quantity of very fertile agricultural land in the deltas of the world would also be lost. All this, however, is highly speculative and there is great scientific controversy going on about these possible effects.

Prospects for Agriculture

The next great possible limitation is in the human use of plants and animals. These are mostly used for food, the importance of which for all living organisms, including humans, can hardly be overstated. For human beings, we have to add fibers which are needed for clothing, bedding, furnishings, and other very significant economic goods. Clothing is virtually unknown in the pre-human biosphere. Most living creatures have the genetic know-how to provide their own integument, and just why the human brain went along with hairlessness is a curious evolutionary puzzle. In almost all human cultures, however, clothing is a necessity.

One worrying thing about the longer-run future is that agriculture, by far and away our most important supplier of food and fiber, has become increasingly dependent on fossil fuels, especially oil, both for energy inputs and even for fertilizer. Certainly a sudden collapse of oil inputs into the United States would create a very major crisis. The combination of a rapid increase in scientific and technological know-how, coupled with the availability of cheap oil, has created an agriculture, especially in the United States, which is unprecedently productive in terms of labor, so that we have been able to release large numbers of people from agriculture who have gone into industry and especially into the expansion of government and the service trades. If agriculture has to become more labor intensive as energy and fertilizer become more expensive, this will withdraw resources from other things. We will almost certainly become somewhat poorer as a result. Here the development of more efficient biomass utilization might be of great importance. If the farmer can grow his own energy to be used much more efficiently than the horse, then this highly productive agriculture may still have a long-range future.

Prospects for Minerals

Another worrying problem for the longer range future would be the very sharply increased cost of many minerals and sources of metals and other elements such as phosphorus. The entropy law as applied to mining of all kinds, has a rather subtle component—that we tend to mine the cheap and easy things first, so that with a given technology, resource exhaustion takes the form of moving to deeper, more inaccessible, more difficult mines, with consequent rise in the price of the product. This can be offset, however, and over the last 100 years it has been more than offset by improvements in technology which acted as a replenishment of the mining potential. How long this can go on, of course, is a very tricky question to which I do not think anyone can give an answer. The time must eventually come, however, when the exhaustion principle prevails and mined materials become ever more expensive. Improved recycling is a partial answer to this problem, but only a partial one, for no recycling can be 100 percent effective. The entropy law as applied to materials states that they tend to become ever more diffuse. The geological processes of the earth have resulted in substantial concentrations of various elements like iron, gold, silver, lead, tin, zinc, and so on, which of course is precisely why we have mines. The impact of societal evolution is to diffuse these concentrated materials over innumerable dumps on the earth's surface, or even more fundamentally to the oceans. Concentrating the diffuse, however, takes energy, and it may take a great deal of energy. We cannot assume too easily that there is an ultimate solution in recycling, except perhaps at a lower level of input than we have now.

Evolution as Postponing Evil Days

In effect what the "entropy school" is saying is that all we can ever hope to do is to postpone the evil day when everything will be gone and all potential will be exhausted, and no amount of temporary recreation of potential can avail us, at least in the very long run. Whether they are right about this we really do not know, simply because we do not know enough about the universe. Even if they are right, however, the postponing of an evil day is a highly productive and desirable occupation, and the more postponement the better. In the wonderful phrase of Malthus, "evil is in the world to move us not to despair, but to activity." The ultimate evil might very well be the entropy principle. Fortunately, the whole record of evolution is that evil days can not only be postponed almost indefinitely, but that development is possible. It must be possible because it happened! There is indeed a time's arrow which points in the opposite direction to the entropy law, although it does not violate it, toward the segregation of entropy, which is in a sense a higher law than the entropy law itself. The entropy school, therefore, takes too long a view, although what it has to say is important and must be listened to. It may indeed stir us to the right kind of activity.

The Economics of the Stationary State

At least a partial recognition of the entropy problem is contained in an economic concept which goes back at least to Adam Smith, that of the "stationary state." For more than 200 years, therefore, economists have been strongly conscious of three possible phases of economic change. The first is what Adam Smith calls the "progressive state," in which capital per capita is increasing, per capita income, therefore, is also increasing and population is almost certainly increasing, although a model of the progressive state could be constructed without a population increase. Economists, and especially perhaps the classical economists, have also been conscious of the fact that the progressive state could not go on forever, and that there were limits, not only to the growth of population but also to the growth of capital. The mechanism which brought the progressive state to an end was a fairly simple one. In the case of population, it was simply that as the population grew, it would eventually reach a point at which real income would decline, mortality would rise, and births would eventually be equal to deaths. In the case of capital, the model was not dissimilar. As capital accumulated, the classical economists, especially, believed that the rate of return on it would fall due to the increasing competition among capitalists, and that this would eventually reach a point at which there was no motivation for the further accumulation of capital. Thus, for both population and capital we have something like a subsistence theory, in that there is some per capita income in the case of population, or real rate of return in the case of capital, at which neither population nor capital would grow, and that as they grow in the progressive state both income and the rate of return decline until they reach their subsistence level, at which no further growth takes place.

This, then, is the second phase—the stationary state. Population simply reproduces itself. There may even be an equilibrium in the age distribution after a while, with enough people dying in each age group (cohort) in the course of a year to make it equal the following year to what the next oldest age group was the year before. Capital likewise reproduces itself. Capital indeed is a population of goods. As these wear out or "die," they are replaced or "born" by production, and here again it is supposed that there can be equilibrium populations of all goods and an equilibrium even in the age distributions. The third phase would be the declining state, at which per capita income and capital were declining, and population may or may not be declining.

Adam Smith is not very warm toward the stationary state. In a famous passage he says, "The progressive state is in reality the cheerful and the hearty state to all the different orders of the society. The stationary is dull; the declining melancholy." John Stuart Mill was a little more cheerful about it and thought that even though population and capital might cease to grow, this would still permit human creativity in the arts and expansion of knowledge and that things might not be all that bad if we did not have to go grubbing to get more commodities.

The problem of the concept of the stationary state is that it assumes essentially that there are no exhaustible resources, at least in the long run. A temporary stationary state is conceivable even while exhaustible resources are being exhausted. But when they come to an end, of course, then the stationary state which is dependent on them will also come to an end. For a long, continuous stationary state we almost have to assume reliance almost wholly on solar energy and on an almost perfect recycling of materials. Paleolithic and perhaps very early agricultural societies at least approximated to this, which perhaps is one reason why they went on for so long in a remarkably constant culture. The use of exhaustible resources begins with pottery and metallurgy. There is absolutely no way of turning pots back into clay, so that recycling is completely impossible and just the fact that the earth has a very large amount of clay rather masks the truth that this is indeed a highly exhaustible, nonrecyclable resource. In the case of metals, recycling is easier, but there, too, as we have seen, it cannot be done perfectly. Even some fairly stationary societies, in paleolithic or early agricultural cultures, have exhausted a potentially inexhaustible resource, for instance, by overhunting and exterminating large game, or by cutting down forests faster than they grow, or in soil erosion and depletion faster than the soil restores itself. The stationary state, therefore, is really not the answer to the entropy problem, though there are societies that have achieved an approximation to it or even have been forced into it. And we may be forced closer to it ourselves as the exhaustibles are exhausted and even in the very long run when we exhaust the potentials of increasing human knowledge.

One sees more hope, therefore, in continuing evolution rather than in clinging to the hope of a stationary state. The biological counterpart of the stationary state is of course the climactic ecosystem, in which all species maintain themselves in their niches as equilibrium populations. Even climactic ecosystems, however, are constantly threatened by changes in the parameters of the system through soil erosion, lakes silting up, climate changes and genetic mutations. Even if we postulate a superclimactic ecosystem which is genetically stable, in which all genetic mutations are adverse, we still cannot suppose that the physical parameters of the system will be unchanged forever. All climactic ecosystems, therefore, and all stationary states are merely way stations on the way to somewhere else. They are only steps, which may however be quite long, in the great staircase of evolution.

Notes

1. Nicholas Georgescu-Roegen, *The Entropy Law and the Economic Process* (Cambridge, Mass.: Harvard University Press, 1971).

2. See especially Jeremy Rifkin, *Entropy: A New World View* (New York: Viking Press, 1980).

3. William Jevons, *The Coal Question: An Inquiry Concerning the Progress of the Nation, and the Probable Exhaustion of Our Coal-mines* (London: Macmillan, 1865; reprinted, New York: Augustus M. Kelley).

4. Erwin Schrodinger, *What Is Life?* (Cambridge, England: Cambridge University Press, 1951).

5. National Research Council, *Energy in Transition 1985-2010: Final Report of the Committee on Nuclear and Alternative Energy Systems* (Washington, D.C.: National Academy of Sciences, 1979; San Francisco: W. H. Freeman, 1980), p. 105.

6. Howard T. and Elisabeth C. Odum, *Energy Basis for Man and Nature* (New York: McGraw-Hill, 1976).

7. Jeremy Rifkin, *Entropy: A New World View.*

8. Matthew 6:34.

9. National Research Council, *Energy in Transition 1985-2010*, p. 5.

CHAPTER 6

The Policy Implications of Evolutionary Economics

Part I

Evolution and the Meaning of Policy

Evolutionary economics is a way of looking at the great complexity of economic and social life in terms of the fundamental concepts of ecological interaction and mutation. It looks at commodities as if they were species in the social and economic ecosystem. This is a somewhat new vantage point from which to look at the facts of economic life. It is still the same old reality, but we are looking at it from a different elevation and have, one hopes, a better vision of the intricacies of its relationships as they spread out over space and time. We now need to look at the implications of this viewpoint for economic policy and, in a larger sense, for social policy in general. One of the consequences of the evolutionary outlook is that we see economics and economic life as a subsystem of a much larger system of social and biological evolution and interaction. Nevertheless, the economic system is a fairly recognizable subset of the total system, with some peculiarities and properties of its own, so there are good reasons for examining it separately, provided that we bear constantly in mind that it is not an isolated system but is part of a larger whole.

The first question then is: What do we mean by policy in general and economic policy in particular? The word policy has two rather closely related meanings, a narrow one and a broad one. In the narrow sense, a policy is a strategy of decision on the part of a single decision-maker.

That is, it is a decision which governs and affects future decisions. I decided to shave this morning, though this is not very much of a decision, because I have a policy of being clean shaven, and my beard grows fast enough so that in order to sustain this policy I have to shave every morning. If I had a policy of growing a beard I would not shave in the morning. In this sense a policy is a decision by which future decisions are judged and evaluated. In this sense all individual persons and all organizations have policies. Such a policy has two functions. One is to economize the decision-making process, which in itself can be quite costly and painful. If my policy is being clean-shaven, my decision to shave is virtually automatic. I do not have a lengthy debate with myself as I look in the mirror in the morning saying, "Shall I shave this morning or shall I not?" I simply stagger into the bathroom and shave almost automatically. On the other hand, no policy is absolutely rigid. If I am spending the day at home and will not be seeing anybody, I may decide not to shave and to shave the next morning when I have to go to work. In this sense a policy is a set of rules which in effect makes future decisions known in advance. Such a rule might take the form that if we have to decide between A and B, we choose A if we perceive C to be the situation and B if we perceive D to be the situation.

Policy as Guidelines and Taboos

We now begin to edge over into the second function of policy, which is to provide general guidelines rather than rigid rules for making future decisions. These, it is hoped, will increase the chance of good decisions and diminish the chance of bad ones. Very frequently policy takes the form of taboos—that is, previous decisions about what the decision-maker will *not* do, thus narrowing the field of decision. There is often great advantage in this, for the narrower the field of decision, the easier it is to visualize the alternatives and to evaluate them. The easiest possible decision is the one where there are no alternatives. This however may be too easy, if it means we have eliminated from consideration some possible alternatives, some of which might in fact have been better if we had taken them into consideration. It is clear that in any given situation there is something like an optimum size of the "agenda" of a decision-maker—that is, the number of alternatives that have to be taken into consideration. If the agenda is too large, the number of choices is too many, and it becomes time-consuming, costly, and painful to evaluate them. Hence we develop taboos which rule out many of them and so narrow the agendas. If we narrow the field too much, however, we may eliminate alternatives that later we might wish we had chosen.

Taboo is a very important element in the moral structure and policies of all societies. We are often not aware of this because we take taboos for granted. There is a very large number of things that we might do that we simply never think of doing. The major difference indeed between a criminal and an ordinary citizen is that the "taboo line" which divides the field of possible choice into the allowable and the prohibited lies much further out for the criminal. The ordinary citizen never decides to mug an old lady and steal her handbag, even though this would be perfectly possible, for the act is on the other side of the taboo line. In the case of the mugger, the taboo line is farther off, though it always exists; even the mugger would probably not mug his own mother, though some of them might. The taboo line not only excludes things we regard as evil but things that might be regarded as too saintly, like selling all we have and giving it to the poor. The taboo line is subject sometimes to quite sudden shifts. This happens to individuals sometimes in a mob. It happens to nations as they shift from peace into war. In peace there are a very large number of things that a nation does not do that it could do. These inhibitions tend to break down in war and the taboo line is pushed a long way out.

Government's Role in Policy; Maximizing Discounted General Welfare

This brings us to the broad meaning of policy, in which we think of it as related to a total society and as being the peculiar responsibility of government. Government is the only agency in the society which has an obligation to look at the total system, to make decisions with a view to whether the system as a whole is moving over time to positions that are regarded as better rather than worse, or as good as can be achieved. In theory at least the government is supposed to act for the whole society and make its decisions with the welfare of the whole society in mind. Its ideal is supposed to be a maximum rate of increase in general welfare, or at least a minimum rate of decrease in the general welfare if the external circumstances are such that a positive increase in welfare cannot be achieved. This welfare must be thought of as a kind of capital good consisting of the discounted sum of perceived future welfares. Discounting is simply the present time equivalent of some future welfare. This present time equivalent is usually less than the expected future welfare for two reasons. One is impatience, the type of perspective which makes people prefer $100 now to $200 in ten years' time, if given this choice. The other is uncertainty. Future welfare is discounted by some kind of subjective probability, so that a prospective high welfare which is very uncertain and improbable will have a low present value.

We might say, therefore, that the object of policy is to set up some kind of a structure which will maximize the present value of expected future net welfares. It is important to look at it in this way; otherwise, we could not possibly understand how decisions could be made which worsen current welfare in the expectation of future benefits. People leave comfortable homes and go through all the agonies of emigration and pioneering, which diminishes their present welfare in the hope of greater welfare to come, the present value of which they estimate to be larger than the present value of their current situation. Similarly, a government may start a war which immediately results in a large diminution of current welfare in the hope of future increases in welfare or the avoidance of future decreases. Rates of discounting tend to increase sharply as we move into the future because of increasing uncertainty, which is why most decisions are made in a relatively short time framework.

Policy as a Decision of the Powerful

In the above argument we have used the government almost as if it were an abstraction. We realize, of course, that if fact government decisions are made by people who happen to occupy positions of power. There is clearly a great difference between the decisions of powerful people and the decisions of not-powerful people. The power of a person can be defined as the size of the consequences of the person's decisions in the system as a whole. The decisions of ordinary citizens affect their own future and the future of the small group around them, usually in a small degree; a decision of a president of the United States may affect the whole human race for good or ill; and there are all shades of power in between. The power of a decision-maker on the whole depends on the place which is occupied in some hierarchy. It is this hierarchical structure which makes the decisions of the president so powerful and the decisions of the janitor unpowerful.

Nonhierarchical Power

Hierarchical power, however, is not the only form of power. There is also influence, the capacity of the poet, the prophet, the novelist, the preacher, the advisor, the scientist to change the images of the people who have hierarchical power and so change their decisions. There are times in human history when this is very important. Jesus certainly had more impact on human history than Pontius Pilate or the Roman Emperor, and Karl Marx probably has had more impact than the Czar of Russia, because of the influence over time which these figures possessed. There is also power which has nothing to do with hierarchy, like the power of inventors. Even in economics, as Keynes remarked, the ideas of the academic scribblers of one generation become the conventional wisdom of the powerful in the next.[1] The extent of power even of the powerful depends also on the size of their agendas. Very often these are severely limited by the organizational structure and the information which comes up to the people at the top, so that their power is much less than appears at first sight, simply because all kinds of people with less hierarchical power lower down in the organization have the power to limit the agendas and therefore the decisions of the people at the top.

Responsibility in the Powerful

When we recognize that it is people that make decisions, not abstractions like the United States or General Motors, we also have to recognize that powerful people may be guided by considerations of their own personal interests rather than that of the organization or the society for which they are responsible. The whole problem of responsibility in powerful behavior indeed is a difficult one. A philosopher king no doubt is the ideal powerful decision-maker, but the chance of getting one in a powerful position seems to be very small. There is indeed a principle which I have called the "dismal theorem of political science"—that most of the skills which lead to the rise to power unfit people to exercise it. If power is passed on by family inheritance, as in a hereditary monarchy, there are no skills at all required to gain power on the part of the king's son, and, indeed, the skills involved in being the son of a good king often make the son a bad king when he inherits the crown. There may be some genetic component in general intelligence, but this is a very poor argument for the hereditary principle, simply because rascality is almost certainly not inherited through the genes but is learned. A clever, good king often produces a clever rascal as a son, and a clever rascal may well be worse than a dull one. This seems to be why the hereditary principle of succession has gradually been abandoned except for ceremonial positions and constitutional monarchs, simply because it is quite incapable of producing people who can handle the increasing complexities of power. Conquest and revolution likewise are poor training grounds for the exercise of the conquerors' power. Conquests usually turn out to be highly temporary unless the conqueror is absorbed into the society in which he has conquered, as in the case of the Norman conquest of England and many conquests of China. Revolutions nearly always turn out to be sour; witness Napoleon, Stalin, and Sukarno.

In spite of all these difficulties there is a surprising amount of responsible decision-making on the part of powerful people. Much of this arises out of personal internal pressures and the sheer desire to do a "good job." Even rascals in power tend to delude themselves into thinking that they are highly responsible and desirable decision-makers. Powerful decision-makers that have no image whatever that their decisions are for the benefit of the larger society are probably quite rare. In addition to these internal factors there are always external factors. Tyrants have a certain tendency to be assassinated, very bad kings to be deposed or to have their power clipped in some way. In democratic societies where legislators are elected, they very frequently want to be reelected and in order to be reelected they at least have to persuade the majority of the electorate that they are in fact behaving responsibly and that their decisions are on behalf of the society as a whole, not for their own personal wealth or aggrandizement. For the powerful as well as everyone else there are "taboo lines" and these may be set internally. President Ford had a much larger area of taboo than President Nixon did, but in President Nixon's case the external environment caught up with him and the external taboo line led to his resignation. He had done things which are taboo for a president and, if he had not resigned, he would almost certainly have been impeached. The very resignation,

furthermore, was the recognition of an internal taboo and it was probably guided in part by his image of himself as a responsible president
who would spare the country harm by resigning rather than being
impeached. This is not to say that personal considerations did not play a
role also. Eventually all decisions of this sort are mixtures of public and
private motives.

The Critique of Policy and the Instability of Error

What is important is that there is a constant critique of actual government decisions in the light of various policy ideals. These may be made
by direct opponents of those in power, with a view to replacing the
decision-makers whose decisions are being criticized, or they may be
made by concerned citizens in what might be called the "public interest"
community like Ralph Nader and John Gardner; or they may be made
by professional scholars and scientists like John Maynard Keynes or
Milton Friedman.

The examination of policy in the large, therefore, is of great importance, for even though the people who examine it may not themselves
be in positions of hierarchical power and authority, if their examination is
a correct one and if we move toward a "truth" in these matters, the influence is likely to be large. There are processes, both in simple systems in
folk learning and in complex systems in scientific learning, which tend
towards the continual elimination of error as time goes on, so that
people's images of the world are likely to have an increasing proportion
of truth. There are sometimes exceptions to this rule. There have been
times when a plausible and vigorous error triumphs and becomes
dominant in human minds. No matter how plausible, however, and no
matter how powerful it may be, error has a fatal weakness, in the sense
that error can be found out whereas truth cannot. It is the asymmetry
between truth and error in the images of the human race that is perhaps
the most basic source of societal and cultural evolution.

Agendas of Decision Widened by Learning

When we look at the evaluation of policy and its associated decisions, however, in the small or in the large, we face two difficult, rather
separate, though not unconnected problems. The first is the problem of
the image of the future itself and realism of this image. All decisions

involve choice among an agenda of alternative images of the future in the mind of the decision-maker. If these images of the future are unrealistic, the decision will not produce the future that is imaged when the decision is made. If I am at the top of a building and want to get down and one of my images of the future is that if If jump out of the window I can fly down, selecting that one will get me into very serious trouble when I reach bottom. Illusions about the future become more common as we move into more complex systems and there are correspondingly more decisions that are regretted. If regret leads to a learning process, however, the proportion of realistic images of the future may increase and of bad decisions may diminish. The learning process of science in all its fields has led to a widening of realistic human agendas and has enabled us, for instance, to send human beings to the moon, which wishing, magic, and pre-twentieth century technology would never have enabled us to do. Whether this has led to better decisions, however, is not easy to answer. It has led to an increase in agendas, but this does not necessarily mean that we choose the right ones.

Evaluation of Agendas and Conformity to a Group Ethos

This brings us to the second problem of decisions, which is the evaluation of different items on the agenda of decision. This is something that we do all the time; indeed we cannot make a decision without it. The critique of evaluations, however, is a more difficult problem than the critique of agendas. The truth of an image of the future is found out by fulfillment or disappointment. It is harder to know what we mean by the "truth" of an evaluation. At least we do in fact evaluate our evaluations; this indeed is what I call "first-order ethics," in which we say either to ourselves or to another, "Your evaluations of the past are fine, or are miserable, and you should have made different evaluations." We can even have an ethics of the second order in which we say, "I think your ethic is miserable and you are criticizing evaluations and preferences by false values." It is not easy to describe in simple terms the processes by which we make these critiques, but they are an essential part of any society. Any group or subculture indeed tends to develop a consensus on these matters, and individuals either conform to this and correct their evaluations towards those of the group or they break out of the group into another one with an ethic that is more congenial to them. Libertarians tend to break out of authoritarian groups, authoritarians out of libertarian groups. Within the larger society there is also a process by which the various consensuses of various groups are evaluated. In our own society we tend to put a high value on the scientific ethic and a low value on the criminal and the nonconformist. But the criminal sub-culture has an ethic just as much as the scientific subculture or religious subcultures.

In evaluating policy of any kind we must have some kind of ethic in mind; that is, a set of preferences which we regard as being more than individual tastes and a standard by which individual taste can be judged; otherwise the whole concept of policy degenerates into conformity to the peculiar tastes of the decision-maker. In the case of powerful policy affecting society at large there has to be some machinery for evaluating various alternative futures even when these are realistic. There is not, however, widespread and universal consensus in regard to these ulti-mate valuation systems, as the gap between the communist world and the free market world testifies, and even the gap between Christians and Muslims in Lebanon or in Cyprus, or between Protestants and Catholics in Northern Ireland. Where consensus breaks down, however, the results are likely to be tragic, for there seems to be in any particular situation a minimum degree of consensus below which the society falls back into violence, to the detriment of all parties.

The Coordination of Values

(1) Prices

There seem to be three rather different processes in society by which values are coordinated. Coordination is not the same thing as con-sensus; that is, we do not all have to agree if in some sense we can agree to differ. But there does have to be a minimum degree of consensus which permits these coordination processes to operate. I have called these coordination processes the "three P's": prices, politics, and preachments. Prices, of course, refers to the market; that is, the complex set of processes by which goods are exchanged, production is specialized and organized, and the resulting income is distributed. Out of the very diverse preferences of human beings in the market network, what emerges is not agreement in regard to preferences, but specialization and a capacity, within the limits of general scarcity, for each person to satisfy the person's own preferences without interfering with those of others; in fact, even helping others to satisfy their preferences.

We see this first in the labor market, where differences in skills, temperaments, and preference for activity can at least partially be satisfied through the choices which the labor market opens up: The outdoorsman becomes a forester, the recluse becomes a monk, the extrovert becomes a businessman, the intellectual becomes a professor, people who like power enter politics, and so on in a vast variety of accommodations of individual temperaments to always limited opportunities. Then the summation of preferences for commodities tends to determine the mix of commodity outputs. If everybody suddenly became a Seventh-Day Adventist, the output of coffee and alcholic beverages would decline dramatically, and people in these occupations would have to find other forms of employment and production. The structure of relative prices mediates this coordination of individual preferences and is affected somewhat by them, though only insofar as changes in relative outputs produce changes in relative costs and in production transformations.

The great virtue of the market is that it economizes agreement. We do not have to agree about what is to be produced; as long as there is a demand for something at a price that pays somebody to produce it, it will be produced. A dramatic illustration of this principle is the separation of church and state and the free market in religion. Earlier societies believed that there had to be consensus in religion, the slogan being "Cuius Regio, Eijus Religio" or "Whoever is the king, his will be the religion." This principle caused an enormous amount of human suffering and persecution and it turned out to be quite unnecessary. The separation of church and state and the resultant free market in religion has relieved the human race of an enormous burden of agreement. When there is a market in religion, all persons can satisfy their own religious taste without interfering with the tastes of others. Furthermore, religion prospers when it has to meet demands for it in a way that it never does when it is enforced by authority and fear. A good example would be the remarkable contrast in vitality between the state supported Lutheran churches of Scandinavia and the Lutheran churches in the United States, where there is separation of church and state.

(2) Policemen

Besides the market there are two closely related processes in society which coordinate the different evaluations of different people. One of these is the political system, symbolized by the "policeman." It is a system based on legitimated coercion or threat. The political system produces the law, the policemen and the courts enforce it. It is this, for instance, which creates the tax system. Most of us pay our taxes only because we would get into more trouble than it would be worth if we did not. On the other hand, most of us are willing to pay taxes as long as everybody else does. The political system provides taxes, government expenditure through budgets, and the system of law and the regulation which limits individual behavior. It also provides taboos and sanctions, that is, prohibitions with an apparatus for punishment if the prohibitions are transgressed.

Any existing structure of taxation, government expenditures, government creation of money, law, and regulation emerges through long historical processes. At any moment it is the result of innumerable past decisions and it reflects in varying degrees the values of present and past human beings who participated in the system. At one extreme we have the tyrant who imposes his own personal values on the system; at the other extreme we have participatory democracy, the Greek city-state or the New England town meeting, where decisions are reached usually by some kind of voting system, modified by mutual persuasion. Between these extremes we have oligarchy at the one end, where a small class in society effectively makes the decisions, and representative democracy at the other, where a considerable proportion of the people vote for presidents and legislatures, who can be voted out of office if they do not satisfy the majority of the voters. In any political system some sort of agreement is necessary, but what we often find is agreement on form and procedure rather than on substance. If a system permits those who disagree to have a second chance, it keeps them agreeing to disagree.

Virtually all economists agree that there are public goods which cannot be provided, and public "bads" which cannot be eliminated by the market. Defense, law, roads, and schools are almost universally regarded as public goods; pollution, crime, monopoly, as public bads, all of which require government taxation. There is much disagreement, however, on where the line should be drawn between public and private goods and bads, and where the line should lie between those private goods which should be left to the market to provide and those which should be publicly provided. We probably have to accept a range of indeterminacy and dispute here.

(3) Preachments

The third process of coordination of valuations in society is the moral and ethical system. This is the process of social criticism of individual preferences. The mechanisms for this may vary from the lifted eyebrow and the edgy tone of voice when a social convention is violated, to the reprimands of parents and teachers and preachers, up to organized attempts to change the ethics of a society through political action, control of the media, and incessant public preaching as we have in China. All subcultures tend to develop an ethos; that is, a relatively uniform system of individual preferences and attitudes. Individuals who violate this either are under strong pressure by other members of the group to conform or they break out of the group into another one. What goes among the Mormons does not go among the Gays, and vice versa.

The larger society imposes ethical pressures on the subcultures within it. This does not necessarily produce uniformity, however, especially in the larger and more tolerant societies. In small societies uniformity is much larger; for instance, among the Hopi. In larger societies there is room for a variety of subcultures as long as the basic "social contract" and the political contract is not violated. Even larger societies, however, have indulged in persecution of nonconformist minorities, and the ethical and the political are constantly interwoven. The ethical movements in a society have a profound effect on political decisions; witness the prohibition or the environmental movements, for instance, in the United States. On the other hand, political structures also have an effect on the ethical system, as we see in the United States the pressures for racial integration. We think of both politics and ethics as continuous, ongoing movements that never reach an equilibrium, but sometimes move toward conformity and sometimes toward variety.

Part II

Evolutionary Theory and Policy

It has taken a long time to state the problem, but now we are ready to ask: What is the contribution to the solution of these problems of the evolutionary approach to economic and social systems? The first and perhaps the most important contribution is the light which the evolutionary model throws on the actual dynamics of social systems and, therefore, on the alternative futures which may follow from particular decisions, courses of action, and policies. The second contribution of the evolutionary model is the light which it throws on the relative importance of plans as over against environments in changing the course of the future. All decisions are intended to change the course of the future. When we talk about policy in the broad sense we mean action directed toward changing the course of the future in a direction that we regard as good or valuable. The most appropriate policy or course of action, as we have seen, is that which makes the present value of the future greatest. If decisions are not to be frustrated and regretted, therefore, it is of great importance to have a realistic appraisal of the impact of any particular decision or policy on the future itself.

This is a very complex problem, but if we look at it in the light of the world ecosystem, moving under a dynamic of its own with constant parameters

This is a very complex problem, but if we look at it in the light of the world ecosystem, moving under a dynamic of its own with constant parameters but also subject at all times to change in these parameters, at least we know what we are looking for. Thus, the famous "Club of Rome" projections of Forrester, the Meadows, Mesarovic and Pestel,[2] are valuable intellectual exercises in that they develop a simple model of the social ecosystems with a small number of variables, but under conditions of constant parameters. Such projections should never be regarded as predictions because we are sure that the parameters of the system will change and change unpredictably. In thinking about the future we have to be prepared for these changes.

Another value of the evolutionary model is that it should warn us against thinking of complex systems like the earth in terms of simple cause and effect. In ecological systems every change will have multiple consequences and we must look for these and never be content with the immediate or the obvious. Every time we change one population by restricting its niche we change the niches of many other populations, and some will increase and some will decrease. As Garrett Hardin has suggested, the first law of ecology is that you can never do only one thing. Furthermore, it is virtually impossible to do only good. Any decision which changes the future will increase some good things, diminish other good things, diminish some bad things, and increase other bad things. The problem of assessment always involves an overall evaluation of these movements to see if the good that is increased and the bad that is diminished is greater than the good that is diminished and the bad that is increased.

Impact Statements

This is why impact statements about particular policies, decisions, and actions are undoubtedly going to be of increasing importance. Environmental impact statements, difficult and ineffective as these sometimes are, nevertheless represent a very important mutation in the whole political information system, and they will undoubtedly give rise to a variety of other forms of impact statements. We need, for instance, distributional impact statements which will throw some light on the question of who is benefitted, who is injured, and who is unaffected by any particular proposal or action. These would often turn out to be extremely surprising because of the great interconnectedness of the system and the way in which the distributional incidence of anything—whether it is a tax or a piece of public expenditure or regulatory legislation or a court ruling—floats around the system in an intricate series of "passings on" and may finally end up in a very different place from what was the intention of the original act.

Time impact statements could also be of great importance, which try to show what the impact of a particular proposal or event is this year, next year, the year after, and a succession of years in the future. Geographical impact statements which would show the impact on different regions and areas are also feasible. Probability impact statements could be of even greater importance simply because a decision under conditions of high probability is likely to be very different from a decision under low probability and greater uncertainty. Under uncertainty it is extremely important that we keep options open for the future and avoid undue commitment. As certainty increases, commitment becomes more reasonable. An important source of bad decisions is delusions of certainty, which may unfortunately be generated by sophisticated information systems.

The culmination would ideally be an overall impact statement evaluating and bringing together all these various parts of the impact. This would be extremely difficult and might have high uncertainties. But it is, after all, the image in the mind of a decision-maker of the overall impact upon which decisions are made. And the more information systems can assist this process, the less likely are bad decisions based on mistaken images of the future. This still does not rule out bad decisions which are made on bad evaluations.

Production and Planning

Another important contribution of the evolutionary model is the light which it throws on the nature of production. There is constant interaction between the "genosphere" of genetic instructions and information and the "phenosphere" of products. As we have seen, these concepts carry through from the biological world into the world of human artifacts and commodities, and I have argued (p. 26) that production is essentially a process by which genetic information or "know-how" is able to direct energy and transmit information towards the selection, transportation, and transformation of materials into the forms of the product. This is the way a chicken is made from a fertilized egg and it is the way an automobile is made from the knowledge structure involved in its blueprints and its plan.

This throws a great deal of light on the relative role of planning and ecological interaction in the total process of the system as it moves through time. The production of a particular product always involves beginning with a plan. This is the genetic structure and the know-how. A chicken indeed is a planned economy beginning with the five-month, or perhaps the fifty-month, plan which is present in the fertilized egg's information structure. This plan may not be fulfilled if accidents or other decisions lead to death, if energy is not available, and if temperatures are not right, or if a number of other environmental factors are not within rather narrow limits. Energy and materials we see as coders of the information and as limiting conditions which may prevent the carrying out of the plan of the fertilized egg. Once the chicken is hatched, the plan as it has produced the mind and body of the chick has in it devices for expanding the limits imposed by energy and materials and providing for learning capacity. The chick scratches for food, drinks water, and gradually learns how to be a hen by genetically induced growth and environmentally induced learning.

Commodities likewise begin in some human head or heads as know-how, which consists of a plan for the future. The plan indeed is a rather restricted form of policy. It tends to define the things which have to be done at each stage in the course of the process, which may allow for a little latitude in recovery if things go wrong.

Lifestyle of Products: Nutrition, Repair, and Aging

Almost all products, whether biological or economic, exhibit a rather similar lifestyle. They nearly all exhibit a moment of birth, when for instance, the chicken emerges from the egg, the animal from the womb, the automobile from the factory. Up to this moment growth and development have been conducted in a narrow and protected environment. After birth the product is launched into the larger world. It is then subject to three major processes: nutrition, repair, and aging. Biological products usually continue to grow after birth until they reach some sort of maturity. Economic products usually do not; they do not have a capacity for self-production and self-reproduction, though one could think of the "running-in" period of an automobile as a kind of child-hood. All biological organisms require nutrition. That is, they have to take in materials, food, and water with which to restore the energy and materials which are constantly being used up in the body. At any moment any living organism has a stock of "fossil fuel" as stored energy in chemical form. The very process of living uses this up and it has to be replaced by an intake of suitable materials. Similarly, there is constant erosion of bodily structure and this too has to be replaced. The processes of nutrition and replacement are probably not fundamentally different from the processes which lead to growth, but in adulthood there is a quasi-equilibrium (homeostasis), when the intake of energy and materials approximately equals the output in mechanical energy, excretion, and erosion of materials.

Some economic products require nutrition; others require very little. An automobile requires nutrition in the form of gasoline and oil, which supplies it with energy and certain essential materials. The gas in the tank is closely analogous to the ATP in the body which stores energy. The painting of a house is a kind of nutrition which restores a loss of materials. Commodities, however, like furniture, clothing, works of art, and so forth, require very little nutrition, apart from a little polish, brushing and cleaning, or at least are not capable of it. Machines require nutrition in the shape of energy input. Many processes require energy inputs to sustain temperatures as well as to do work.

Repair differs from nutrition mainly in its irregularity. Most biological organisms have a capacity for some forms of self repair, the healing of wounds, and in some cases the growth of new limbs, the restoration of new connections in the damaged brain, and so on. The processes have a great deal of similarity to the original processes of production and indeed can be considered an extension of genetically organized production. In the biological organism they involve the genetic information system and its capacity, again, to direct energy and materials. In economic products repair is very important. Practically no economic products have any capacity for self repair, but human beings, as they are indeed the genetic structure of commodities, are also able to repair them, as they can also improve on the repair of biological organisms through tree, animal, and human surgery. The automobile repair shop has many similarities to the surgeon's operating room in the hospital. Repair frequently involves the replacement of parts which again are produced, however, by almost the same process that produced the original parts. The parts of economic products are a good deal more separable than the parts of biological products. There seems to be no exact biological equivalent to the assembly line, although there is undoubtedly assembly in the egg and in the womb, but it takes place continuously with the formation of the parts, something we have not yet achieved in economic production.

All products are subject to aging as a result of the inherent instability of all complex organizations. Aging is an example of the generalized law of entropy, that every process starts off with potential which is gradually used up. Nutrition and repair eventually break down and the organism dies or the product is scrapped. Products, however, are constantly produced (born) to replace those that die. Biological organisms have the capacity of self-reproduction by division or by sex. Economic products, as we have seen, are produced by the interaction of large numbers of social species and the genetic material is contained not in the product but in the knowledge structure of the human race.

Know-how, Not "Labor," the Main Factor of Production

This view of the nature of production does have important implications for economic policy structure and organization. It is not "labor" that produces a commodity or product, as Marx and indeed Adam Smith and Ricardo thought, but human knowledge and know-how, operating through institutions which enable this know-how to capture energy and rearrange materials. Labor, in the sense of what is bought with wages, is a highly variable mixture of the three real factors of production. It involves some know-how, the ability to follow instructions, and the response to emergencies. It involves a little muscular energy, though as an energy producer the human body is quite small and inefficient and is not capable of producing very much, though it can transport materials and assist their transformation into products. The laborer is also a human body consisting of certain materials which requires nutrition and repair and is subject to aging and death and requires replacement by new births.

The Organization of Know-how

A very important principle of economic production is that the know-how which is the foundation of it is not held in any single mind but is scattered among many minds and has to be coordinated through processes of communication. This is a problem which does not arise very much in biological production, as all the know-how necessary to produce chickens is presumably contained in the fertilized egg, whereas the know-how required to produce an automobile is scattered among hundreds of thousands of people and has to be coordinated. This is done through organization. It essentially is a system of orderly communication among role structures, a role being a kind of node in the communication network with a characteristic pattern of inputs and outputs. Alfred Marshall[3] indeed wanted to put organization as a fourth factor of production; this was an important insight, though it makes much less sense when it is simply added to land, labor, and capital.

An organization is a species of human artifact and is perhaps the most important example of a larger category which, using a phrase of Marx, we might call the "relations of production," which includes all the interactions among different social species, including human beings which are involved in processes of production. It involves, for instance, exchange, as when a highly integrated bundle of know-how, energy, and materials called the worker is hired for a wage; when land is rented from its owner or bought; when money is obtained by the sale of financial instruments such as promissory notes, stocks, and so on, all of which are promises to pay money later. The relations of production also involve a great deal of reciprocity or informal and noncontractual exchange. A worker, for instance, is hardly ever hired to do something which is contractually completely specific. There has to be a good deal of self-monitoring, desire to do good work, willingness to participate in the ongoing life of the organization, and so on, as well as monitoring by foremen. In labor bargaining the employer gives status as well as the money wage and various benefits of belonging to an organization, and the worker gives willingness to participate as well as specific contractual obligations.

Exchange always implies the institution of property, for exchange is always a mutual transfer of property. In labor bargaining, for instance, the employer transfers money and perhaps other things which he owns to the worker; the worker transfers time and activity to the employer. He would not be able to do this unless he owned his own mind and body. Under slavery, for instance, the slave is not paid a wage, but maintenance, for the slave is the property of the owner, not very different from a domestic animal. This is perhaps the main reason why slavery lost legitimacy and hence virtually disappeared.

Centrally Planned Versus Free-Market Economies

The largest question of economic policy at issue in the world today is undoubtedly the choice between centrally planned economies of the communist type and the free-market system. This dichotomy hides enormous differences within the two sides. China has a very different system from Russia, and certainly India is enormously different from the United States. Nevertheless, even if we ranked all the economies of the world in order of similarity, we would find a substantial gap between, say,

Yugoslavia (which is perhaps the least communist of the communist countries) and West Germany (which is perhaps the most socialist of the free-market countries). A critical difference lies in the legitimacy of the capital market, which is virtually denied in communist countries but is asserted in varying degrees in the free-market societies. The issue here is really the optimum balance between single, budgetary, planned organizations and ecosystems bound together by the market. The chicken, as we have seen, is essentially a planned economy, whereas the woods and the fields and the oceans are essentially a free-market ecosystem without central organization or planning. In biological evolution, the determining factor seems to be the diseconomies of large scale beyond a certain point, so that each type of organization tends to have an optimum size.

The largest optimum size for a living organism is still far less than the total quantity of living matter, so that biological evolution does not produce just one organism. There are good reasons for this besides the diseconomies of scale, which have so far prohibited any organism larger than the blue whale. There is also the problem of the precariousness of a system and its capacities to sustain catastrophe. If biological evolution had produced a single organism and it had gone wrong, that would have been the end of it. As it is, the biosphere has extraordinary resilience because it is an ecosystem not an organism. This is perhaps the strongest argument against communism. A communist society is a "one-firm state" in which if anything goes wrong, everything goes wrong, and in which there is an enormous concentration of power, centralization of decision-making, and the capacity therefore for making extremely catastrophic mistakes, as indeed Stalin made in the first collectivization of agriculture and Mao seems to have made in the "Great Leap Forward" and in the "Cultural Revolution." On the other hand, the degree of centralization must not be exaggerated. In the communist societies individual families have a degree of freedom in their expenditures and even their movements. Peasants have private plots and there is a great deal of undercover, surreptitious market activity without which indeed the system would probablly have collapsed long ago. The information requirement of planning increases more than exponentially as the size of the planned organization increases. It is not surprising, therefore, that communist societies are brontosauruses, inefficient in their operations and repressive in their politics. The only way of economizing agreement if there is no market is by tyranny. Even though the tyranny may be well intentioned, it is still tyranny and always has the frightening potentiality of going extremely sour because of the absence of political checks and balances.

On the other hand, the market economy is also subject to certain pathologies which can only be cured by the application of politics in government and perhaps preachments in ethics. Left completely to itself the market economy may produce a degree of inequality in both welfare and income which cannot be legitimated. This is because of the famous "Matthew principle" quoted in the Gospel of Matthew: "To him that hath shall be given." Equality in a pure market society is unstable because the random forces of the market will make some people richer than others; that is, the lucky ones, and the richer will be able to save more easily than the poorer, so that the rich will get richer and the poor will not. This tendency is offset to some extent by luck; that is random- ness, which the fluctuations of the market introduce. Beyond a certain level of inequality, the fact that the rich can lose their wealth by bad luck or bad management and the poor can gain wealth by good luck or superior management offsets the Matthew principle, so that there may be some equilibrium of inequality of wealth. At this level, however, inequality may be perceived to be too great. Hence, government inter- venes to redistribute income or wealth and provide a social inheritance in the form of free public education, welfare payments, social security, negative income taxes, inheritance taxes, and so on.

Competence and Incompetence in Government; Price Policy

Within both the communist and the free-market world there is a prob- lem of policy as between competent government and incompetent government. There is great difference, for instance, between the relative competence of Yugoslavia and the cruel incompetence of Cambodia within the communist countries. In the free-market world, also, there are very wide variations of competence between, for instance, the extraor- dinarily competent, redistributive but not very regulative economy of Sweden, which has brought Sweden in a hundred years from being one of the poorest countries in Europe to being almost the richest country in the world, and the extraordinary incompetence of Uruguay, Argentina, and Chile, which actually succeeded in reversing their economic development in the mid-twentieth century.

Incompetence in government takes two major forms. One is intervention in the price system in such a way as to discourage innovation, encourage ineptitude, and create implicit grants to the undeserving. This is quite easy to do. We have done a fair amount of it even in the United States. Arbitrary changes in the price structure can produce shortages and surpluses and can disorganize the whole relations of production. On the other hand, by no means all price intervention is adverse, though the benefits are often unintentional. Thus in the case of the United States, agricultural price supports had unintended consequences, both favorable and unfavorable. These undoubtedly redistributed income towards the richer farmers, which was not the avowed intention, but by diminishing price uncertainty these measures encouraged investment and technical change and helped to produce a remarkable increase in agricultural productivity. Uncertainty is indeed a very much neglected factor in social policy. If it is large enough, as in the European Dark Ages when bandits roamed the countryside, nobody makes any improvements, capital is converted into treasure and hidden in the ground, and there is no economic development. In modern societies the uncertainties of government produce something of the same effect, so that those who have the power to innovate, provide employment, and conduct useful enterprises, prefer not to do so but to hold their capital in safer if socially less desirable forms. The niches of the enterprising and innovative people shrink, and those of the conservative and the repetitive open up. Market economies are vulnerable, in that they need security in order to operate. Yet radicals who oppose them can easily create the insecurity which makes market operations almost impossible, and we end up with tyranny in one form or another. This is one of the unanticipated consequences of radicalism.

Unemployment and Inflation

Another defect of market-type economies is their tendency to fall into unemployment and less than capacity output. This is something for which there seems to be no easily visible parallel in the biosphere. It may be that there are biological ecosystems which underutilize their resource base in terms of energy and materials because of some failure in, say, the nitrogen cycle, or because of some empty niche in the system which the processes of mutation have simply not filled. The absence of anything that looks like a labor market, exchange or a price system in the biosphere, however, makes the form of this phenomenon extremely different from what it is in social systems. Niches for commodities are created by demands. It is possible for the whole system to produce at undercapacity, simply because if it produced at capacity there would be too large a gap between production and the purchases of goods by households, resulting in continual unwanted accumulations of inventories of certain kinds of goods.

The problem is, of course, much more complex than can be outlined in this very brief account. In a society where there is a private labor market there is a very intimate relationship, as we have seen earlier, between the volume of employment or unemployment and certain dislocations that may take place in the financial system. When an employer hires an employee, the employer gives up money (the wage) in return for a change in his real asset structure which the work of the employees produces; whether this is turning wheat into flour by grinding it, or flour into bread by baking it, or bread in the shop into bread in the household by delivering it, and so on. If there is a rise in the net worth of the employer as a result of this activity net of the wage paid out, then it will be worth his while to do it, though only if this rise is greater than the increase in net worth he could gain by putting the money spent for the wage out at interest. Employing somebody, therefore, means the sacrifice of interest for the hope of profit. If the profit is uncertain, as it usually is, whereas the interest is fairly certain, we would expect an employer to hope for something larger in the way of profit than he could receive in interest. Thus it is not surprising in 1932 and 1933 in the United States, when profits were negative and interest was absorbing 11 or 12 percent of the national income that unemployment was 25 percent. It is surprising indeed that it did not go to 50 percent. In that period almost any employer who hired anybody was either a fool or a philanthropist, for he could usually have done much better by putting his money out at interest. It was only habit indeed and perhaps the hope of better times and an unwillingness to sacrifice existing organizations that kept the economy functioning at all. Whether we could get into a similar situation in the future is perhaps improbable, but the probability is not zero.

This is something that we have to think about in advance and devise defenses against.

This relates also to the fact that historically unemployment has been very strongly related to *gross private domestic investment*—that is, the gross increase in the stock of all goods in the hands of businesses before allowing for depreciation. These consist partly of inventories; short-run cycles in employment have been largely the result of fluctuations in inventories. They also consist, however, of so-called "fixed capital"— buildings, machines, land, plantations, and so on. It is fluctuations in the increase in these things which have been the major source of large depressions, such as that of the 1930s. For the last 30 years, gross private domestic investment has been remarkably stable as a proportion of the gross national product, partly perhaps through habit, the fact that we do this year very much what we did last year; partly perhaps through luck. If there is a sudden sharp decline in the willingness of businesses to add to their stocks of fixed capital, as happened in the early 1930s, then unless drastic offset measures are taken we might again find ourselves in a position with rising and uncontrollable unemployment.

It is hard to think of anything in the biosphere that corresponds to the phenomenon of deflation and inflation, simply because there is nothing in the biosphere to correspond to money. Deflation is destructive to market economies because it destroys profits, without which it is very hard for a profit system to operate. In socialist economies, simply because of the absence of free contracting at privately determined prices, it is easier to control inflation, although it is significant that the freest of the socialist economies, Yugoslavia, has had an even worse inflation than most of the capitalist countries, so that inflation may be the price of market freedoms under any system unless we increase our political skills for handling it. Market economies still have not solved the dilemma of unemployment and inflation, perhaps because we have failed to analyze sufficiently the real phenomenon of the labor market, and especially have tended to take the employer for granted. The heterogeneity of the labor market in a country like the United States makes the problem of full employment much more difficult than it is in Sweden, with its relative absence of minorities.

Policies Toward Distribution

A good deal of political and ideological controversy revolves around policies toward changing the distribution of wealth and income as the social process goes forward into the future. That the government has some power to do this there is no question, though how great is its power is a matter of considerable debate. At one level of abstraction we could say that government has the power to redistribute economic rents, though how to identify these and even after they are identified how to capture them is a largely unsolved problem. The pressures for redistributional policy are a function of the political structure, and especially of the political security of government itself. Legislatures which are elected on a regional basis develop very complex processes of regional exchange of distributive favors under the name of log-rolling. Furthermore, allocation and distribution are very closely intertwined and it is hard for government to do anything which does not affect the allocation of resources between uses and the distribution of income among persons. Perceptions of injustice or distributional inequity affect political behavior, though it is often hard to separate this from the log-rolling effect.

Subsidies to agriculture, for example, are almost universally defended on the grounds that farmers are poorer than the rest of us with comparable skills and capital and that there is something unjust about this. Hence, we have had agricultural subsidies and price supports of various kinds in many different countries. These policies almost always have side effects which frequently turn out to be much more important than the specific objective of the policy. Thus, in the United States, agricultural price supports by reducing uncertainty in agriculture—and in effect subsidizing the rich farmers much more than the poor ones—led to a remarkable upsurge of technical change and investment in agriculture after 1933, which resulted in a massive transfer of some thirty million people out of agriculture into the cities, thus helping to create the urban problem, but which also permitted a substantial increase in the production of non-agricultural goods and services, even though there is some evidence that a good deal of what was released from agriculture was swallowed up in government, the product of which is highly dubious.

Direct subsidies to the poor—such things as food stamp plans, welfare payments, and so on—are characteristic of all modern societies. This does not reflect perhaps the political power of the poor, which is not very great, partly because they are a minority in a rich society, and also because they tend not to be politically mobilized. It reflects rather a sense that poverty, especially visible poverty, is a "public bad." It diminishes the citizen's sense of pride and identification with his nation, is regarded as something that is shameful politically; hence, one can get a good deal of support for a "war against poverty" or its equivalents. A war against poverty seldom seems to be won by the poor, but that again is a matter of unexpected and unforeseen consequences.

Public education may well be the most significant anti-poverty policy insofar as it provides a public inheritance beyond the family and also increases that know-how which leads into productivity. The impacts of the labor movement, for instance, in pressing for universal free public education in the late nineteenth century, may have had a much greater impact on the distribution of income than anything which the labor movement did in terms of monopoly power and collective bargaining for a few crafts constituting the labor aristocracy.

On one issue there is wide agreement among economists—that attempts to redistribute income through manipulating the relative price structure are costly in terms of allocational inefficiencies and often succeed in redistributing income to the wrong people. We have to distinguish here between stability in price structure as we have seen above in agriculture, which may be distinct gain through the reduction of the unnecessary uncertainties of the free market, and manipulation of the average relative price structure itself, through, for instance, rent control.

Evolution as Progress

We have not come out with a single and simple answer. The evolutionary process is immensely complex and we understand it very imperfectly. This, however, is what the world is like and, if we try to interpret it in terms of simple dialectical processes, in terms of struggle, conquest, and revolution, we will wholly fail to understand the complexities of the real world. A good policy is not easy. It involves information systems considerably beyond what we have now and also institutions for rapid feedback and correction of mistakes. The evolutionary perspective, however, does open up the possibility for very large improvements in public policy based on more realistic appraisals of actual futures corresponding to various decisions, and also on an evolutionary learning process by which "bad" values are slowly reduced, even as error is reduced in our images of the world, and as biological evolution eventually produced the human race, simply because in all ecosystems there is likely to be an empty niche at a higher level of complexity but not one at a lower. If there are empty niches there is always some positive probability that they will be filled by mutation. It is these asymmetries which give direction to evolution, both in biology and in social systems, and give us hope for improvement.

One should not be ashamed of a belief in progress. It is painfully slow and intermittent, interspersed with catastrophes and reversals, but there is a strong case for believing that in the long run it is built into the system, provided there is not an ultimate and irretrievable catastrophe. We should never forget, however, that from the human point of view progress is improvement in the state of persons. Everything else is an intermediate good. Unless society improves the production of persons, no matter what it may produce in terms of material artifacts and social institutions, what is going on is not progress. We can go to the moon and explore the universe, we can become even richer than we are now, we can get rid of war, disease, poverty, until everybody dies at a ripe old age and with full possession of their faculties, but if in the interval we have not, by well-judged and well-criticized human values, increased the quality of life of persons, it is not progress. It may be indeed that we will produce our evolutionary successor. No species has ever lasted more than a few million years, and with the tremendous acceleration of the evolutionary process under the impact of the human race, it could well be that the human race will last a much shorter time than that. We are only a blip in the great history of the universe, but it may be a very significant blip, for we do represent an extraordinary acceleration and intensification of the evolutionary process. If we produce a successor that is in some sense even by human values better than we are, with a larger biogenetic or noogenetic potential, then the human race itself, like those individuals of it who have fulfilled their potential, can depart in peace.

NOTES

1. Keynes is quoted in William Breit and Roger L. Ransom, *The Academic Scribblers: American Economists in Collision* (New York: Holt, Rinehart & Winston, 1971), p. v: "... the ideas of economists and political philosophers, both when they are right and when they are wrong, are more powerful than is commonly understood. Indeed the world is ruled by little else. Practical men, who believe themselves to be quite exempt from any intellectual influences, are usually the slaves of some defunct economist. Madmen in authority, who hear voices in the air, are distilling their frenzy from some academic scribbler of a few years back."

2. Jay W. Forrester, *World Dynamics* (Cambridge, Mass.: Wright-Allen Press, 1971); Donella and Dennis Meadows et al., *The Limits to Growth* (New York: Universe Books, 1972); Mihajlo Mesarovic and Eduard Pestel, *Mankind at the Turning Point* (New York: E. P. Dutton/Reader's Digest Press, 1974).

3. Alfred Marshall, *Principles of Economics*, 9th ed., C. W. Guillebaud, ed. (London and New York: Macmillan, 1961).

INDEX

A

academic scribblers, 172, 195n.
acid rain, 162
adaptability, 104-106
agenda field, 98
agendas
optimum size of, 170-172
widening of, 175-177
aging, of products, 184
agricultural
development, 71, 130-133, 144, 151
prices, 115, 190, 193
productivity, 136, 140
prospects for, 162-164
Alchian, A. A., 105, 122n.
Allee, W. Clyde, 18, 21n.
alternative costs, 58-62
Argentina, 189
automobiles, 26, 30, 36, 54, 184-186

B

bathtub theorem, *11*
behavior, maximizing, 97-104
bioevolution, *12*
biomass energy, 161, 164
bottleneck problem, 118
Boulding, Kenneth E., 47n., 122n.
Brahe, Tycho, 139
Breit, William, 195n.
budgets, 41, 119
Burns, Robert, 19, 21n.
Butler, Samuel, 45, 47n.

C

Cannon, Walter B., 122n.
carbon dioxide problem, 162

catastrophe, 14, 108, 150, 188, 195
capital accumulation, 79, 166
centralization versus decentralization, 137
centrally planned versus market economies, 19, 40, 121, 145, 187-189
China, 20, 75, 109, 146, 174, 180, 187
civilization, period of, 68, 127, 134-136
climactic ecosystems, 55, 87, 106, 167
climate effects of changes in, 163
cobweb theorem, 95
coevolution, *30*
coffee production, 61-63, 178
colonizing mode, 106
commodities, *47-81*
communism, 106
versus capitalism, 40, 80, 145, 177, 187
convergent evolution, 44
Copernicus, 137, 139
Crusoe, Robinson, 123
cyclical systems, 95

D

Darby, Abram, 141
Darwin, Charles, 18, 21, 32, 83, 122n.
de Chardin, Teilhard, 154
deer and beaver, 59
demand and supply curves, 87-96
development
and evolution, 85
as niche expansion, 68
differential rates of, 77
dialectics, 20, 42-44, 84, 86, 96, 194
diamonds phenomenon, 35, 99
dismal theorem of political science, *173*